MOUNTAIN TOP
Experience

CAMP MARANATHA
IDYLLWILD, CALIFORNIA

CELEBRATING 50 YEARS OF MINISTRY

MOUNTAIN TOP
Experience

Compiled and Edited by
JODY BEGGS REEVES

WINEPRESS WP PUBLISHING

© 2003 by Jody Reeves. All rights reserved.

Printed in the United States of America.

Packaged by WinePress Publishing, PO Box 428, Enumclaw, WA 98022. The views expressed or implied in this work do not necessarily reflect those of WinePress Publishing. The author is ultimately responsible for the design, content, and editorial accuracy of this work.

No part of this publication may be reproduced, stored in a retrieval system or transmitted in any way by any means, electronic, mechanical, photocopy, recording or otherwise, without the prior permission of the copyright holder except as provided by USA copyright law.

Unless otherwise noted all scriptures are taken from the Holy Bible, New International Version, Copyright © 1973, 1978, 1984 by the International Bible Society. Used by permission of Zondervan Publishing House. The "NIV" and "New International Version" trademarks are registered in the United States Patent and Trademark Office by International Bible Society.

Scriptures marked TLB are taken from The Living Bible, Copyright © 1971 owned by assignment by Illinois Regional Bank N.A. (as trustee). Used by permission of Tyndale House Publishers, Inc., Wheaton, Illinois 60189. All rights reserved.

Scriptures marked NASB are taken from the New American Standard Bible, © 1960, 1963, 1968, 1971, 1972, 1973, 1975, 1977 by The Lockman Foundation. Used by permission.

"They'll Know We Are Christians" composed and arranged by Peter Scholtes. © 1966 F.E.L. Assigned 1991 to The Lorenz Corporation. All rights reserved. International copyright secured.

ISBN 1-57921-454-1
Library of Congress Catalog Card Number: 2002101497

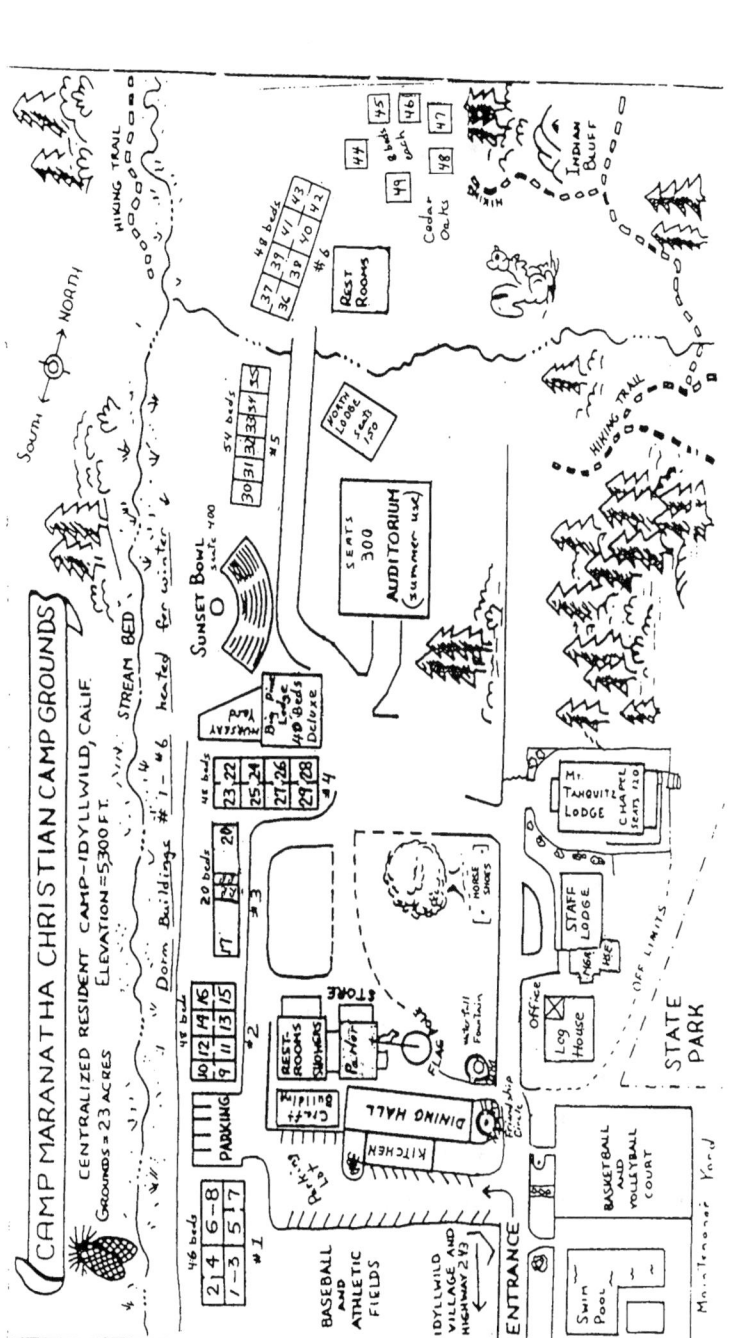

Mission Statement

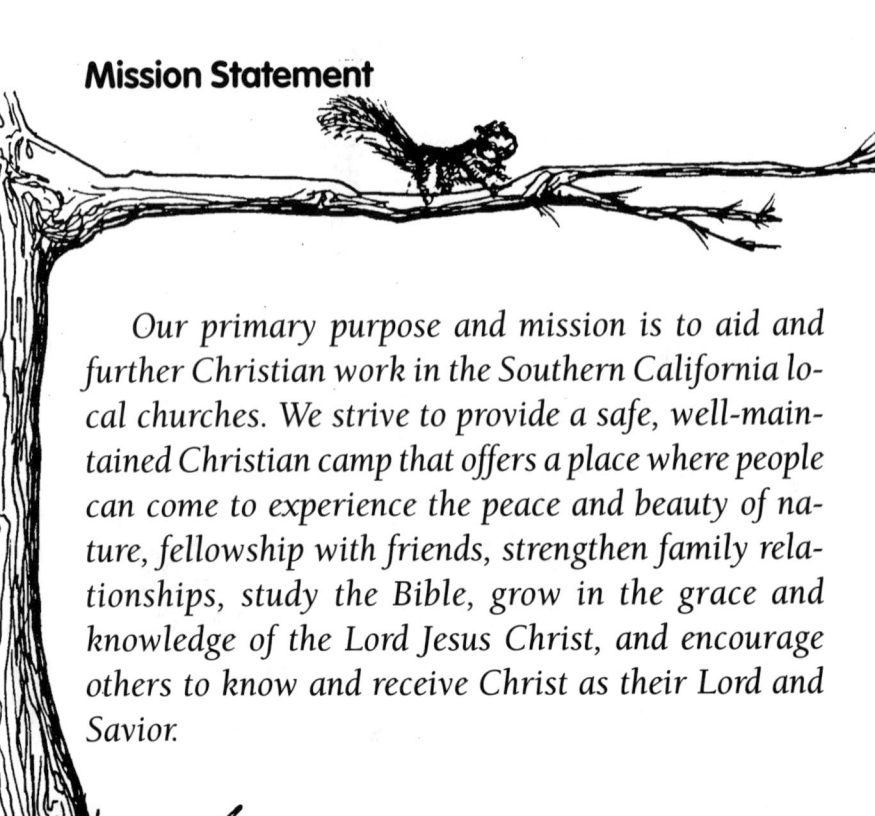

Our primary purpose and mission is to aid and further Christian work in the Southern California local churches. We strive to provide a safe, well-maintained Christian camp that offers a place where people can come to experience the peace and beauty of nature, fellowship with friends, strengthen family relationships, study the Bible, grow in the grace and knowledge of the Lord Jesus Christ, and encourage others to know and receive Christ as their Lord and Savior.

Camp Maranatha is owned and operated by the Advent Christian Conference of Southern California.

Camp Maranatha is one of the original members of Christian Camping International and has been active in that organization since 1955.

Dedication

This book is dedicated to our Shepherd, Who leads us beside the still waters, makes us to lie down in green pastures, and restores our souls.

Remember that story in the Bible about the man who owned a hundred sheep?

Remember how one of the sheep wandered away and the man left the ninety-nine sheep on the hills to look for the one that wandered off?

Remember how he searched and searched for that lost sheep until he grew impatient and said:

"What's one stupid sheep to me? I have ninety-nine good sheep who stay where they should. Why should I care about this one sheep who foolishly wandered off and got himself into trouble?"

Then he went back to his good sheep—the ones that hadn't wandered off—and he put on his robe and slippers and drank a cup of hot cocoa by the fire.

Remember that story?

Neither do I.

"In the same way your Father in heaven is not willing that any of these little ones should be lost." Matthew 18:14

Acknowledgements

The whole thing started on an autumn afternoon in 2000. My mom—who is really big on ideas—had an idea. I have to admit, it sounded good. I mean, after fifty years, there had to be many stories about Camp Maranatha and it would be fun to put some together in a little anniversary memory book. The next thing I knew, I was very busy (a common effect of being in close proximity to Nancy Beggs when she gets an "idea"). In the midst of soliciting and reading submissions, contacting printers and publishers, and projecting costs and time schedules, I began to have some ideas of my own. This would be no ordinary memory book. No, this would be a polished, professional literary tome of grand proportions. This book would make Camp Maranatha a household word across the nation—no, the world. Yes, imagine the foreign language editions!

What you hold in your hands is neither a little anniversary book nor a professional literary tome, but something in between. Once I received the go-ahead from the Director (Dick Beggs) and the Camp Maranatha Operations Committee (thank you for approving and even encouraging me in this endeavor), more than a hundred people sent in their stories of Camp Maranatha experiences. Countless others participated in fifty years of building the memories from which these stories and illustrations are drawn. In addition

Mountain Top Experience

to saying a sincere thanks to all those listed in the contributor's section at the back of the book, I would like to make special mention of a few "volunteers" who served as proof readers, (um, you capitalized "Dining Hall" fourteen times and left it lower case twelve times), research assistants (can *anyone* find out what "Old Man" Richardson's first name is?) and chairperson of the illustrations committee (okay, Jody Crimi, I guess you figured out there really wasn't a committee—you *were* the committee).

   A great big thank you to Nancy Beggs, Cary Bursvold, Kevin Beggs, Allison Donahoe-Beggs, Ashly Reeves, Jody Crimi, Katie DeRoche, Keith Shirley and Bobbi Crawford. Special thanks also to Liz (Dobbs) Favela and her parents, Bill and Vera Dobbs for allowing us to use images from their rubber stamp company free of charge.

   Here's a big hand for everyone who helped take *Mountain Top Experience* on the journey from an idea to an actual book.

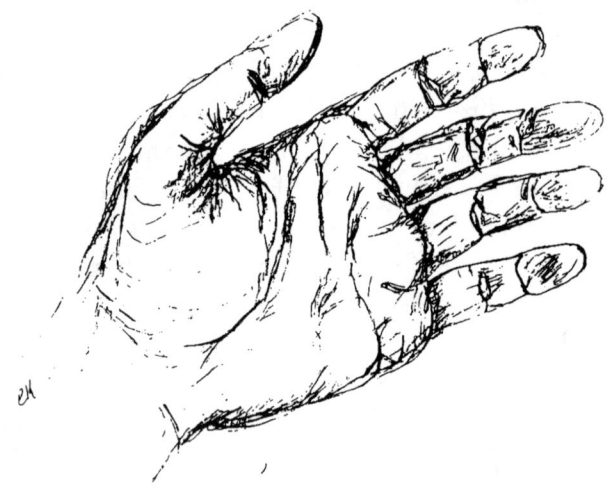

(Hope you don't mind a little corny camp humor.)

Table of Contents

Introduction xiii
1. The Early Years 15
2. I Remember 29
3. Family Camp 37
4. Camp Couples 49
5. People We Recall 57
6. Teen Camp 75
7. Service 93
8. Guest Groups 111
9. Kids Kamp 121
10. Poet's Corner 137
11. Camp Staff 149
12. Lessons 181
13. Songs & Skits 203
14. Nature 219
15. Impact 225
    Conclusion 245
    In Honor 247
    About Our Contributors 255
    Index 273

Introduction

Imagine the winding mountain journey. Drive on through the town of Idyllwild and continue past the familiar Camp Maranatha sign. The ballfield on your left may be a dry and dusty brown, it may be dotted with clumps of struggling grass—a perfect environment for twisted ankles and impossible softball hops—or it may rest snugly under a blanket of fresh, sparkling snow. It will appear the way you remember it. Walk from the parking lot through the friendship circle. Take a look at the fountain and pause a moment to listen to the mountain water splash against its river rock sides. For some, the fountain and even the friendship circle may be new additions since your last visit. Others can't imagine Camp Maranatha without them. Either way, continue along the path by the dining hall, snack bar, cabins, A-frame . . . Your friends are waiting.

When you open the pages of this book imagine night has fallen. You are one of a group gathered around a carefully-laid fire at the sunset bowl. Sparks fly high into the night trailing up toward a myriad of stars, their radiance unhindered by the smog and bright lights of the valley far below. Firelight flickers upon friendly faces as each one tells the tale of Camp Maranatha. You may not recognize every name, you won't remember every story—you may even remember some of the details quite differently, but you will know you are among friends in a place that will always, in one way or another, belong to you.

Welcome home.

The Early Years

A gray squirrel chatters amiably, dashes across the green summer grass, and winds his way around a tall pine in pursuit of another bushy-tailed creature. The tree is one of many that oversee the grounds of Camp Maranatha. This particular pine gazes from lofty heights upon the blindingly bright tin roof of Camp Maranatha's dining hall. A small herd of children scurries by dragging beach towels and raising dust with feet not quite pushed all the way into damp and dirty flip-flops. The snack bar is open and the children hurry lest they arrive just after the heavy wooden windows are swung into place and bolted shut.

Pastor Johnson* follows the little gang with his eyes as he rehearses—strumming the opening chords of tonight's first worship song. His mind drifts back home where the girl he met six years ago sits rocking their three-week-old son. This is his tenth year at Camp Maranatha. It is the place where he met Jesus, the place where he felt that strange pull into ministry, the place where he asked that girl he misses to be his wife. Only ten weeks of his 27 years have been spent on this piece of earth, yet it is his camp.

Pastor Rick Johnson is not alone in this feeling of ownership. He is only one of the thousands who have lived and loved in this place since 1951. Many have experienced the awakening of their conscious mind to a God that loves them. They have laughed joyfully and cried away the sins of the past in pine-scented splendor. Only a very few know of the series of "chance" encounters that worked together in the origin of Camp Maranatha. And that is just as well. Those who are ignorant of the events that occurred fifty years ago are no less blessed by their camp experience. Even so, for those of you who are curious, we hope you will enjoy this version of Camp Maranatha's history. Some may remember it differently. Some details may be missing or imprecise, but we hope we have not lost the heart of the story in the intervening years.

*Pastor Johnson is a composite of many who have visited Camp Maranatha.

Mountain Top Experience

The Advent Christian Conference of Southern California had been holding camp meetings at Camp Carlsbad in Carlsbad, California, beginning in the early 1920s. The beach property ran alongside the railroad track and the highway. The only permanent building was a kitchen/dining room.

Ed Jaffarian, a building contractor from New England, had moved his family and his business to Pasadena at the end of World War II. As a member of the Pasadena church, he wanted to improve the camp and offered to either build an auditorium on the grounds at Carlsbad or help the conference find another campground. Soon Ed began taking a group of conference representatives to various locations under consideration. One of these was four to five miles off the Ortega highway and so primitive it didn't even have water. Another was between the Cajon Pass and Big Bear Lake. It had been a monastery and had some basic facilities. They also looked at a piece of land in Garner Valley (between Anza and Idyllwild).

It was after looking at the Garner Valley site that the men noticed the sign to Idyllwild and decided to follow Highway 243 to the small mountain village. Entering Idyllwild, they stopped at a real estate office and met Jerry Johnson. When asked if there might be some property in Idyllwild suitable for a campground, he took them to a tract of land which had been used for a saw mill. There were five buildings on the property: a large two-story building (the original Big Pine Lodge), an office building (now remodeled as the Snack Bar and Ice Cream Parlor), a three bedroom home (used as a residence for the first manager, it is now called the Staff Lodge), a smaller one-room building with a fireplace (the original Ponderosa), and a mill shed.

"There's an $11,000 mortgage on the property and the owner needs an additional $7,500 to start a business. I think

The Early Years

he would take $18,500 for this," said Jerry, indicating the surrounding 20 acres.

"Let's see if he will consider selling for $17,000," said Ed, writing a personal check in that amount. "We would like a written response in the next few days."

A few days later, Ed informed Frank Scott, Conference President and Pastor of the Tustin church, that the conference now owned a beautiful piece of land in the San Jacinto Mountains—though he never would say if the original offer was accepted or if he had to pay more.

Jerry Johnson also handled an adjoining tract of about 3.5 acres, which includes the ball field. At a later date, he offered it to the conference for $3,000 saying he had turned down $5,000 for it as he disapproved of the way it would be used. The conference officials thought it would be a nice addition and bought it even though they were a little skeptical about the $5,000 offer.

Years later, when Errol Hunt was talking to the local dairyman, the man commented that he offered Jerry Johnson $5,000 for that tract of land so he could expand his dairy and that Jerry refused to sell to him. We used to think the stables and their rodeos were inconvenient neighbors when they occupied the area where the lumberyard and county road department are now located. How would you like to have a dairy covering the ball field, half the dining hall and half the area for the cabins of Building #1? Let's hear it for honest realtors!

Not everyone was pleased with leaving the beach in Carlsbad. A few still say it was a mistake and those who were there cherish fond memories of those camp meetings at the beach. One notable opponent to the camp in Idyllwild was Pastor Osborne of the Los Angeles church. He referred to it sarcastically as "the Camp in the Sky." It must be said,

Mountain Top Experience

however, that once he had a chance to visit the site, he changed his tune and became a great supporter.

The first camp meeting was held at Camp Maranatha in 1951. Most of the people stayed in tents. The Tabernacle (tent) from Carlsbad was used as a meeting place. The dining hall was under construction. One end of it was used for eating while the other was being roofed. When the roofing of that end was finished, it was used for eating while the other end was being completed.

Errol and Juanita moved to Camp Maranatha in 1951. Errol was chairman of the Board of Trustees of the Tustin church during the building of the present parsonage. That had provided him with experience in securing surplus government property, which he put to good use in obtaining much of the original equipment and building materials for the camp. He seemed to be the man for the hour to get the camp ready for use and was selected by the conference as camp manager.

No one in our group could recall who the speakers were for the camps in 1951 and 1952. Rick Drew, the new pastor of the San Diego church, was the speaker for 1953. Carl Fromhold was the song leader. Meetings were still being held in the big tent from Carlsbad.

The camp manager reported directly to the Conference Board of Trustees until the conference decided to appoint a Camp Management Committee with its own treasurer as a more efficient way to manage the construction and operations of the camp.

To the best of our collective memory, we know Leroy Connelly was on this original committee and served as long as he lived. Others who were probably on the committee include Sim Draper, Al Schmekel, Chuck Anderson, and Adlai Bowden.

The Early Years

Volunteers did almost all the original construction and preparation of the grounds. Roy and Estelle Peterson, of Los Angeles church, did much of the work on the cement block buildings. They had many helpers whose names we wish we could record. We do remember that Roy built the circle around the flag pole. Some members of the Anderson family of San Diego built the fireplaces in the Dining Hall and Ponderosa.

Prepared from tapes of a conversation between Errol and Juanita Hunt, John Palmer, and Walter Shirley that took place about 1990. Errol and Juanita were the managers of the camp from the time it started in 1951 until 1971.

The following contributors share their memories of Camp Maranatha's early years.

1952 was our first full summer in Southern California. Dorothy and I had been married the previous August in Eugene, Oregon, following my first year at Fuller Seminary. She was the Sunday School Superintendent for the Pasadena Church and I did the pastoral calling while Interim Pastor, Dr. George Ladd, did the preaching. We had visited Carlsbad Camp Meeting briefly in the summer of 1950 while on the way home from a month-long trip following my college graduation in Massachusetts. We were very excited at the prospect of attending Camp Meeting in Idyllwild. But the scary thing was that we were asked to be Camp Father and Mother for the youth.

As I remember it, L.A. Pastor Ronald Bezanson was the evangelist, Tustin Pastor Frank Scott was Camp Director, Colton Pastor Bill Bailey was cook, National City Pastor Leon Bohy and Pasadena Pastor George Ladd and his wife were teachers, and Pastor Chet Rice was the director of recreation and song leader. In spite of the heat and the dust

Mountain Top Experience

and our having to live in very cramped tent quarters and having full responsibility for the youth, it was a great camp. How blessed we were to see many of the young people make decisions for Christ. During the altar calls, we were thrilled to see newly born-again youth slip out of the tent to kneel in prayer for their unsaved friends. The results caused much joy in heaven and on earth.

On the last day of Camp Meeting, the youth showed their appreciation by presenting us with a very useful gift: a wicker picnic basket and a service-for-six set of stainless flatware with polished wood handles. This brought tears to our eyes, and even now I can see the shy smiles on their faces. Termites long ago demolished the basket, but the flatware is still in the silverware drawer, and Dorothy chooses those forks to test her vegetables and as her preferred implements for eating. Yes, God is good. We thank Him for prompting Ed Jaffarian to make the gift of the land in Idyllwild, and for giving the Southern California Conference the faith and the gumption to develop Camp Maranatha into the splendid campground that it has become. To God be the glory through Jesus Christ our Lord.

Austin Warriner

Growing old has one advantage. You pile up a stack of memories that bring joy and an appreciation of God's goodness. Christian camping has played a very significant part in our lives. Both Betty and I were baptized in the slough beside the old coast highway at prior camp meetings (at the Carlsbad site). My first real job was setting up camp under the direction of "Old Man Richardson" and Clarence Campbell. We lined up the platforms and erected the tents for housing the families who came from our conference churches.

The Early Years

The wonderful gift of the beautiful property in Idyllwild by Ed and Ruby Jaffarian and the first Camp Meeting in 1951 were a mixed blessing for some who missed the good times at the beach. Errol and Juanita Hunt presided over the first twenty years of camp development with the assistance of many volunteers.

Serving on the Camp Management Committee with Roy Connelly, Sim Draper, Phil Shuman, and others was a great privilege. Frank Scott was Conference President and had a lot to do with naming the grounds Camp Maranatha.

Bob and Betty Crimi

Bonnie: Ed, didn't you work on staff before I did? If so can you remember the dates and the people you worked with?

Ed: Wow! That was a long time ago. I worked part of the summer that we put the roof on the dining hall. Besides doing some of the roof, I hauled trash to the dump. I remember that I didn't have a driver's license yet, but Errol Hunt let me drive the WWII-surplus Ford Jeep and trailer down the highway to the dump. The thing was constantly stalling, and I remember hitching a ride back to camp on one occasion. Probably I was about 15 years old, which would have made that 1950 (plus or minus a year or so?).

I can't remember reliably who I worked with. It was likely some of the usual suspects: Dave Bohy, Earl Wright, Irv DeVoe, etc., but I'm not sure my mental images of them relate to staff activity or the camp programs.

Bonnie (Pitts) Froehlich to her brother Ed in e-mail conversation

Mountain Top Experience

Back in those days, I enjoyed the early morning trips to the dairy in Idyllwild to pick up our milk, dairy products, and ice. I also remember the trips for supplies we made at times—down the mountain to the little town of Hemet—and how good it was to get back, because Hemet was always hot. At that time, Hemet was just a very small community, nothing like the size it is now. Several years ago, I rode through Hemet for the first time in years and could hardly believe this was the same place.

Ken Steinseifer

I think I must have attended the very first camp in Idyllwild. Some of my earliest memories include me pitching a fit while my mother removed a large splinter from my leg, my grandmother being irritated with me for getting pitch on myself, and my younger sister catching lizards while they pitched the tent for the tabernacle (their tails came off—the lizard's, that is).

Cindy (Howard) Bailey

My earliest memories of camp include the long driving trip from Tustin up through the Santa Ana Canyon, through Riverside, past March Air Force Base and through miles of fruit orchards in Hemet . . . and on up the mountain to Idyllwild.

As most people know, the camp was originally a lumber mill, and I fondly remember the property as it looked at the very beginning. I remember our family visiting Errol & Juanita Hunt and their family, and Errol becoming the first camp caretaker.

In the early years I have many fond memories of the lumber mill buildings and equipment. Memories of staying in the Big Pine Lodge and the old missionary cottage with my family . . . playing on the big tire swing in a pine tree

The Early Years

near the missionary cottage. At Family Camp and Kids Kamp we slept in war surplus tents and attended services in the tents also—those big army green tents. We caught big june bugs and stuck them in other kid's sleeping bags ... then sat back and waited for their startled reactions! We caught lizards and had great nature hikes.

My most memorable recollection was of our first year of family camp in the concrete block buildings. My brother Ray and I were in the bunk beds (I was 13, Ray was 9). When I woke in the morning, Ray was on the floor (instead of in the upper bunk)—he was knocked out cold with a big goose egg on his head from falling out of the top bunk during the night! I woke Mom and Dad (Roy and Hazel) and they woke Ray. He was okay, just had the big lump on his head!

John Connelly

After invitations to Family Camp, work weekends, and women's retreats, we finally decided to come to a camp clean-up, because if we worked our stay was free—a very attractive feature for a family adjusting to one income.

"Where is this camp?" we asked.

"Well, it's in Idyllwild—at the stop sign turn right and follow the road. You'll see a sign that says Camp Maranatha."

"Oh, I went to a Camp Maranatha once. I wonder if it's the same one."

We were greeted by someone named Dick Beggs. We choose a room in building 3. That will be more comfortable for a couple with a young child, and room 21 was available. Boy, this sure seems familiar. I remember staying in a room with bunk beds made of cement blocks like these buildings are. I wonder if there is an old telephone pole around here somewhere. I remember watching a light bulb explode when it was rained on. Well, there is an old pole

Mountain Top Experience

over there. Let's see, that old building over there looks a lot like the building where we had meals. I wonder?

After looking around for a while, I asked Mr. Beggs a few more questions he was happy to answer.

"Yes, we do rent to other church groups in addition to our own denomination."

"Yes, the camp was moved here from Carlsbad around 1951."

"Yes, we did rent to the American Sunday School Union."

It was the Camp Maranatha I attended as an 11-year-old kid. Melva Barth and I figured I attended in 1952, the year after the camp's birth. We used the Big Pine Lodge for meals—there was a long, narrow room with tables and benches, a big kitchen with a big stove, and one bathroom with one shower and a long line. There was a big tent tabernacle we sat in for our meetings, services, and choir practice. I was lucky. I was in a building, but my friend slept in a tent. A lot of kids were sleeping in tents. A new building was under construction and we weren't allowed down there (the Dining Hall). I wondered where the boys went to the bathroom. This summer of 2001, Melva told me that the men used a bathroom upstairs—now I know (49 years later)!

Jeannie Davis

I was lured to Camp Maranatha by my Aurora College roommate Bonnie Pitts (Froehlich). Having been hired by Erroll & Juanita Hunt, it was my good fortune to spend the summer of 1960 working as a lifeguard and running the snack bar. Nicknamed "Schultze" by some of my co-workers, the snack bar that year became known as Schultze's Shack.

It was a wonderful summer for me, my first in Idyllwild. I've always had a special attachment for Idyllwild and have

The Early Years

been back many times to visit. I always take time to drive over to the campground and see what has changed.

Judy (Hall) Menish

The man you call Ed Jaffarian was always "Uncle Buddy" to me. As a boy in the 1930s, I visited with the Haverhill Jaffarians almost every summer, and my favorite memory was Aunt Ruby's ice cream cones. My younger cousin Myron, Uncle Ed's son, tagged along with another cousin, Dickey, on some of our youthful adventures.

My uncle Buddy had been in a number of businesses from his youth. When he first left school he earned money repairing bicycles. At one point, he owned a shoe factory, but the thing I remember was my dad lecturing his brother about things like "demon drink."

It was in 1944, at the end of World War II, when my dad and I were visiting Haverhill that Uncle Buddy announced to my dad that he had accepted Christ. We were in the basement of the family home at 58 Bateman Street in Haverhill, and I remember to this day the happiness of the moment for the two brothers.

At the time, my uncle had been working in construction camps as an employee of a contractor who was tearing down old army camps. As a new Christian, he refused to work on Sunday and was fired. It was then that he started building houses out of used lumber. He had told my dad that he and God were partners and that 50% of everything was to go into God's work. In 1945, the family moved to California and the rest of the history can be better told by Bob Crimi, Walt Shirley, John Palmer, and the others who were involved with the church conference of Southern California at that time.

Jeff Jaffarian

Mountain Top Experience

I came up with my dad (Harry Pitts) who was on the Camp Committee when Mr. Jaffarian showed this property to offer it deeded over to the conference. There was a lot of snow on the ground, and it had the old Two-story House where the new motel building is, the old residence that is now the Staff Lodge, and the Missionary Cabin (Ponderosa) with only a dirt floor (unfinished).

Bonnie (Pitts) Froehlich

Camp Maranatha caught my attention in the early to mid 1960s, when one day at a commission meeting I heard one of the conference officers make a remark that shook me up.

"We could sell Camp Maranatha, invest the money, and send every one of our Sunday school kids to any camp they chose to attend, using only the interest from the investment."

Until then, I had taken the camp for granted. I was content with attending Family Camp, promoting attendance of the other camps by our Sunday School kids, and providing them transportation to and from camp.

It was common knowledge that the camp was having financial problems. Even though I wasn't sure that the officer was serious about this suggestion, it shook me up. The camp was not just a place to send our kids for a week each summer. Ruth (my wife) and I were raising three boys with the hope and intention that, when they were old enough, they would want to work on the camp staff during their summer vacations. We felt sure there could be no better environment for their first experiences away from home than working at camp under the supervision and protection of Errol and Juanita Hunt. Without Camp Maranatha that would be impossible.

The Early Years

So, we started looking for ways to get more involved with the camp. At that time the A-Frame had been under construction for too long and progress was stalled after several volunteers had exhausted the time they had available. We started pushing for completion of the A-Frame and, as so often happens to people who get "involved," it wasn't long before I found myself on a committee. I was appointed to the Camp Management Committee and accepted the position of chairman a year or two later.

Walt Shirley

Errol and Juanita Hunt were the resident caretakers at camp and I was a teenager on summer staff. One week Danny (Meeker), one of the other staff members, had fallen in love with a camper from whatever camp was in at the time, an eighth grader as I remember. At the end of the week, when the campers went home, Danny became inconsolable with loneliness. He asked for someone to drive him to her house, but found no one. When bedtime came, all staff members were accounted for but one. Danny was missing, and although he'd been heard to swear that he would walk down the mountain in order to be reunited with his new love, we assumed he was somewhere around the grounds. Sure that he would show up eventually, we all went to sleep.

By the middle of the night, however, Juanita had worked herself into a fit of worry. She woke Errol and insisted that he round up the staff guys and organize a manhunt. Since Juanita would not be put off, Errol came down to the staff cabin with his flashlight and told us all to get dressed. Informed of our mission, and rubbing the sleep from our eyes, we followed Errol down the hill, along the road, and into the back door of the Dining Hall. Once inside, Errol retrieved a five-gallon tub of ice cream from the freezer, set it

Mountain Top Experience

on one of the stainless steel counters, and invited us to get bowls and to help ourselves. We then sat around in the kitchen and passed a pleasant while talking, laughing, eating ice cream, and listening to Errol tell some of his justifiably famous stories and reminiscences of camping days gone by. When an acceptable amount of time had passed, Errol returned the ice cream to the freezer, looked at his watch, and said, "Well, boys, let's go back to bed. We've looked for Danny long enough."

Barry Tate

I Remember . . .

Mountain Top Experience

*Trying to recall special moments
of my camp experience
is like opening the flood gates.
The memories pour over me
like a rushing river
cascading over a mountain ledge,
falling into a reflective pool.
There the memories ripple out
in ever widening circles
until they reach the shores
and anchor me once again
to the warm embrace
of countless friends.*

Debbie (Peckens) Hammond

I Remember . . .

Although I do not keep in touch with anyone except Dick and Nancy Beggs, and Keith and Paula Shirley, the friendships I made at camp are etched in my heart. I remember names of many of the campers and staff as if it were just yesterday. I remember hikes up the mountain and then riding the tram down. I remember the summer we had a fire on the mountain. I remember swimming laps, and laps, and laps, and playing water basketball in the pool. I remember cleaning cabins and bathrooms, cooking on the griddle, wiping tables, serving food, running "Norman," and being the lifeguard. I remember sleeping in the Two-story House—my home for three summers. I remember the work weekend when Pastor Jim (Smith) slept, or tried to sleep, in the cabin next to us. He would not let us sleep on the ride home because we had kept him up all night! I especially remember Jack DuFour for all he did for us youth. I remember talent shows with goofy skits and songs (Rah, Rah, Potatoes and Ham!—*see Songs & Skits for lyrics*). I remember not ever wanting to miss a chance to head to camp. I have very fond memories of Camp Maranatha and I am glad that my children had the opportunity to visit at least once, and that I have been able to return several times.
Carol (Peckens) Laroche

One of my best memories is watching as Kevin (Beggs) learned to make fried rice—a lot of fried rice.
Tricia Zimmerman

I remember . . .
. . . sneaking into the boy's staff cabins early in the morning with Carol Aulis (Muska) and getting caught.
. . . playing football at a retreat and having my picture printed in the AC Newsletter.

Mountain Top Experience

. . . hikes to Dead Man's Cave with Barbie Smith (Taylor).
. . . hikes to Tahquitz Peak, getting my Squirrel card, and riding the tram into Palm Desert.
. . . Kids Kamp, Teen Camp, and Family Camp.
. . . riding to the county dump with Dave Crimi. (A real treat!)
. . . celebrating my 10th Birthday in the Big House with the Crimi Family on an October weekend. (Getting my first hula-hoop and taking home a black baby kitten from the Hunts.)
. . . eating *Frosted Flakes* in the dining hall late at night with my mom (Marie Drew), pouring on the milk, and watching ants swim to the surface of the bowl.
. . . taking my boy friend, Phil (Miller), to Maranatha to help Nancy and Dick at weekend camps.
. . . making friendships that have lasted a lifetime.

Debbie (Drew) Miller

Funniest Memory goes to Bob Barth for the time he ate 50 boxes of cereal.
Honorable Mention goes to Dave Crimi—Hey! I still haven't forgotten you made me chase peacocks off the baseball field!!!

Kathy (Hahn) Bottom
AKA Chicken or Rooster

I remember early chilly walks all the way to the "lavs" after leaving a cozy sleeping bag.

Carol (Aulis) Muska

I remember the old Big Pine Lodge . . .
There were winter weekends with a group from the Pasadena church. Sledding into the gully was exciting to say

I Remember . . .

the least. Summer events in that building hold memories of teenagers "sleeping" upstairs while older campers tried to sleep downstairs. I remember climbing out that upstairs window onto the porch roof and leaping to the ground in the middle of the night more than once. Sneaking back in up those rock stairs with the wobbly wood railing without waking any of those senior citizens was always a much bigger challenge. Years later I hosted a women's retreat in that building with the ladies from Idyllwild Community Church.

I remember pool time . . .

For several years there was no pool at camp. At swim time we were loaded onto the big stake-bed truck and driven to another location where we spent the afternoon sitting on the concrete deck, covered with baby oil, frying in the sun. When we finally had a pool of our own, I spent many painful hours learning how to do a "jack knife" dive. Little did I know how many times in the future Dick and I would empty, scrub, paint, and refill that same pool in preparation for our summer guests. However, by far the most significant event for us at the Camp Maranatha pool has been the joy of witnessing the baptism of each of our three children and our oldest grandchild.

I remember the Sunset Bowl . . .

Another spot that holds lots of significant memories is The Bowl. I remember singing "Great Chief" and "Do Lord" with flames leaping higher than was safe or smoke finding me no matter where I sat. Years later, I sat in that same bowl watching our children (Jody, Cary, and Kevin) and then grandchildren (Brian and Ashly) participate in the closing ceremonies as each of them attended Kids Kamp. I was a counselor at Kids Kamp for several summers. Each of our kids in turn were counselors, and this last year we watched our granddaughter, as a counselor, present the Little Chief Award to a camper in her cabin.

Mountain Top Experience

I remember . . .

. . . learning Bible Verses that I can still recite today.

. . . late night pranks and getting in trouble with my friends (mostly ministers' daughters).

. . . hiding from the camp director when I was supposed to be in bed.

. . . almost getting sent home after telling what we thought was a really funny joke.

. . . Saran wrap and peanut butter, wintergreen mints sparking at night.

. . . clothes on the flagpole.

. . . "round the building you must go."

. . . hiking for a "squirrel card."

. . . volley ball.

. . . round table ping-pong.

. . . friendships that last a lifetime, and memories that never end.

. . . the bell ringing as we drove away from camp.

. . . crying all the way to Mountain Center.

Nancy (Crimi) Beggs

I will never forget "green clouds," Nair (oops), rearranging furniture (yes, indoor furniture can become outdoor furniture from the staff boys' rooms), many episodes of undies up the flagpole, *embarrassing* moments at the pool during Family Camp (some memories best to be forgotten!), "Dini, put your pants on and get away from that boy!" blaring over the camp loudspeaker (thanks, Zann [Gustafson]) because I was late to work and we weren't allowed in the kitchen with shorts on, "Rah, Rah, Potatoes and Ham," pool parties (fully dressed in the middle of the day), middle-of-the-night Snack Bar raids, shaving cream fights, and *many* more memories that will remain forever locked in my heart and mind.

Dini (Walters) McGregor

I Remember . . .

I went to camp with my Grandma (Lillian) Koehler, as well as a slew of other relatives: brothers, sisters, cousins, aunts, and uncles. I have made many friends whom I'll never forget, although we may not keep in touch. These are people who hold my fondest memories of growing up.

I remember when my sister, Beth, was on camp staff and someone tricked her into going into the upper boys bathroom to clean it. She entered the bathroom not knowing that a counselor (for the camp that was in progress at the time) had just gotten out of the shower. I think Beth learned to knock after that. My favorite camp story about Beth is when they tied her to a bed frame and took it into the showers. That is how she earned the nickname "wet head."

Gwen (Koehler) Marron

1960, we bought a pickup with a camper shell and went to General Conference in Washington. Soon we found the camper most useful for transporting any kids from the Advent Christian Church in Pasadena who might need rides to Kids Kamps, Teen Camps, and mid-year retreats. Those were the days before seat belt laws, and what an experience just to go to camp!

Ruth Shirley

Special memories of Camp Maranatha—manning shovels and picks to dig a trench around the Hunt house during a major deluge; the "wonderful" smells and dust from the corral next door to the pool; birds on the roof and in the tree branches next to the mission house where Bonnie Pitts (Froehlich) and I were housed; singing duets with Roger Parolini in the Tabernacle and County Park; meeting many wonderful Advent Christian friends and acquaintances; throwing my leg up over a horse and ripping the seat out of

Mountain Top Experience

my pants, then having to tie a shirt around my waist until I could discreetly remedy my difficulty; the time Jerry (Davis) and Kenny (Steinseifer) put a frog in the cash register at the shack (Snack Bar)—wasn't I surprised when I rang up a sale?; walks to town to see a movie each week; the hikes to Tahquitz Peak and having to run down the mountain on one hike because darkness was descending.

Judy (Hall) Menish

I loved Camp Maranatha. I remember meeting a lot of friends, singing in the local church choir on Sundays, doing a lot of goofing around, a lot of swimming, and liking a lot of American girls. I remember Vickie Kuhn from Santa Ana, Linda Flora, Jana Mosgar, Carol Connelly, and, of course, Bonnie Pitts Froehlich with whom I am still in touch every year. I liked American girls so much I married one! Still married to the same girl for thirty years!

Nghiem and Sherril Phan

Family Camp

Remember when a family was a father and a mother gathered around the dinner table with their children—maybe with a maiden aunt or a widowed grandmother, as well? Remember holding hands and giving thanks to God around that table? Remember going to church all together and staying for a potluck afterwards? Remember packing up the family and heading to the mountains for a week or ten days of camp meetings?

These may be recent or distant memories. Some may have only read of such things in books or seen them on reruns of The Waltons. But regardless of the changes in family structure and lifestyle over the years, there are still families who make a week together at camp a priority in their lives. Whether you are a mom or a dad, a child or a grandparent, the words that follow may remind you of the reasons why Family Camp was important to you last century, last decade, or last year. Perhaps, they will give you reasons to come and find out why Family Camp is still important today.

Mountain Top Experience

Camp Maranatha means so much to me that words are not sufficient. The memories I have are too many to list. The things that camp and its people represent to me are so wonderful that I get too emotional to write without shedding tears. I came to my first Family Camp in 1988 when I was pregnant with my second child. Dave Tapley was the first person I got to know there. How surprising to find a young man who was so nice to fat pregnant women. Another memorable encounter was while I was on a hike to suicide rock. A very nice man named Andy Smith stayed back to see if I was all right. He thought for sure I was going to have that baby on the spot. He and his wife, Sylvia, have been my friends ever since, along with Smitty (Knechtel), too.

Denise Stiers

I remember being in the Family Camp choirs directed by Carl Fromhold and Roger Parolini. And I'll never forget eating Good and Plenty candy from the snack bar with Gene Crimi and sneaking out of the evening vespers services together.

Debbie (Drew) Miller

Teen Camp and Family Camp contained some of the more hilarious adventures in my camp memories. At Family Camp some amazing things happened:

One morning all the chairs were found bowing down to worship God.

During a water fight, Dini Walters (McGregor) was after someone who ran into the girls bathroom. She was shocked to find the person she opened the door on and doused with water was my grandma (Lillian Koehler). Grandma still fondly remembered "Water Bags."

Family Camp

Louia Gransee might recall being director and having some "Fine Looking Ladies and Strange Looking Boys" arrive at dinner and give him a big kiss. I still hear his sympathetic pastoral voice saying, "My heart pumps peanut butter for you."

I remember Katie Jaffarian saying, "Turtles, turtles, oh . . . turtles," as her father (Jeff Jaffarian) caught a group of us talking very late at night in the Ponderosa.

One moment in time that marks my grandma's great oratorical skills was when she took her turn speaking at chapel representing the La Verne Church. Tustin had been represented the day before. The key to Tustin's presentation was the great fount of history as presented by their oldest member, a woman named Fanny. Grandma's opening remark the next day was, "We don't have any Fannies in La Verne." God only knows what the rest of the speech was because we were all laughing for a long time. Some may still be laughing.

Ellen Koehler

Camp Maranatha has been a blessing to me. There were many years that, as a single parent, it was important to have a place to bring together my children from three mothers. Maranatha made this possible. My cynical spirit was tolerated, and love was extended to my entire family and the occasional friends that joined us for Family Camp. The prayers of my friends and family have not gone unrewarded. At the age of seventy, I have accepted Jesus' sacrifice for my sin.

Jeff Jaffarian

I remember sleeping out in the "boonies" with other young people, wonderful music, combined choirs.

Carol (Aulis) Muska

Mountain Top Experience

There are lots of memories old and new, serious and funny. But as I reflect on the early days, I remember another significant event. At a Family Camp evening service one summer, the speaker gave an invitation to commit to a life of full-time Christian service. I was about fifteen years old and without hesitation made my way to the front of the Tabernacle. I can remember being very sure that whatever God had for me to do, I would gladly do it.

Of course at the time I had no way of knowing that thirteen years later He would bring me and my family back to Camp Maranatha for a life of full-time Christian service. These past thirty years have been filled with wonderful memories also. Dick and I could not have asked for a more blessed, fulfilling life. Thank you, Lord, for calling us to serve at Camp Maranatha. And thank you, Camp Maranatha, for being a place of "joy and love."

Nancy (Crimi) Beggs

In 1953, we packed our family of two boys (Dwight and Ralph), ages one and three years, for our first Family Camp experience. Reverend Rick Drew was the speaker for camp, and we well remember some of the stretching sermons he preached. When Walt saw what our camp had to offer to a family, including our beloved Carl Fromhold as choir director, he was ready to seek employment in Los Angeles. By August, 1954, we were settled in California.

Family Camp became a regular part of our vacation. We had some meaningful times. Walt and I offered our time to help in the Bible School programs. The kids taught us much, and we found the evening services very inspiring.

In 1956, Keith was born to us, and you guessed it—when he was barely walking, he joined his brothers Ralph and Dwight, Grandma Edith Mushrush, and me at Family

Family Camp

Camp. Walt came up on weekends. Keith was easy to control that year as he had a push toy that went everywhere with him, allowing him to walk on the uneven ground. When I'd go in search of him, I would often spot the push toy first, and he was always close behind.
Ruth Shirley

In 1969, my first husband died. While in mourning, I drove to visit my relatives in Massachusetts and attended the church in Brockton. My Uncle, Gardner Howard, was quite active there. That summer I went with my grandmother, Della Mansfield, to camp in Santa Cruz, California. Then I went to Maranatha. I remember Mr. Drew, the Smiths, Knechtels, Gransees, Pitts, Shoemakers, Crimis, Hunts, Joe Tom Tate, and many others.

A couple of humorous things I recall as an adult in Family Camp were Lillian Koehler saying she was "twice the woman" she was at Aurora, and Dave Crook telling someone who had asked how old his daughter was, "How do you expect me to remember? It changes every year!"

I loved helping Jeannie and Otis Davis care for the children during Family Camp. Jeannie told me once that my son, Micah, was the only child who ever escaped while under her care.

I love Maranatha because it is such a beautiful place and full of good memories and old friends. One feels closer to God there!
Cindy (Howard) Bailey

I was raised in a small church in a desert community, and when I was around nine years of age, I went to my first church camping experience against my father's wishes ("She's too young"). I was hooked. Pine Valley, Camp

Mountain Top Experience

Maranatha, Cedar Glen, Tahquitz Pines—I never knew where any of these camps were, except I knew Pine Valley was near San Diego. My goal in life, at age twelve, was to somehow be a permanent camp counselor.

When we first went to Family Camp, it wasn't very convenient for mothers with young children. We all had to leave the meetings with our restless children as they could not sit for two to three hours at a stretch. I saw the playground and asked why we didn't have a program for children five and under? The answer was there was no one to do it.

I was on leave from a children's center where I had taught two to five-year-olds and had a baby of my own, so I knew how to take care of infants. That was the beginning of our service in Family Camp as the providers of child care. Our son, Charles, and later our daughter, Mary, were in the young children's program when they were small. Then, when Mary was six, rather than moving on to the next age group, she began training to help us. She was, and still is, excellent with infants and young children. As she grew older, I often left the infants in her care. Since we many times had fifteen to twenty-five children, she was a great help. Otis looked after the play yard, Mary took care of the infants, and I provided the Bible stories, crafts, music, and whatever else was needed.

I have only missed two Family Camps in all these years. The first was when Otis was on a business trip and I had a beautiful eight-month-old daughter, as well as a three-year-old son to care for. I felt I couldn't handle all the children at Family Camp, too—especially without Otis. I did, however, bring my kids up for the weekend (this was when Family Camp ran from Sunday to Sunday). The other time I was unable to provide childcare was when I was staying

Family Camp

with my mother after my father's death in June. Otis and Mary ran the program without me that year.

Now, our granddaughter, Samantha, is coming to Family Camp with us. Samantha's first experience was as a four-month-old infant. She has come all eight years of her life and this year is asking about Kids Kamp. We will do almost anything to be here at camp. While we have not been able to listen to many of the speakers or sing many songs at Family Camp, we have been deeply blessed to be able to be part of Family Camp using the skills God gave us. Otis' quiet manner has calmed many a fussy baby or child. Mary's love of babies and toddlers has richly blessed her here. Charles helps in the play yard and learned that children do the same things each year—like building sand castles and throwing sand. I have been richly blessed. Thanks to Dick and Nancy for the hospitality they always showed and for the many needs they looked after for a particular person who runs the child care program.

I guess, in a way, I have become a camp counselor—once a year during Family Camp for 25 years—half of Camp Maranatha's life.

Jeannie Davis

I have a few memories of the firsts I experienced at Camp Maranatha. The most important to me was the first time I realized the importance of God, and I asked Jesus to be my Savior. I was very young and it was actually at Family Camp after a meeting in the Tabernacle that I really felt God's presence and knew I needed Jesus to be saved. Quietly, I asked God to be with me. As each year passed, every one felt like a rededication to that moment. We all have fallen away from God and sooner or later come back to him. Most of the time, for me, it was at camp—I mean the coming back part.

Gwen (Koehler) Marron

Mountain Top Experience

I came to love Jesus at Camp Maranatha. I made friendships that will last my lifetime, too. I don't need to list the names, because you know who you are! Last summer, I was able to attend Family Camp and bring my own two small children. Those children were just dreams to me when I was a teenaged camper. But now they are an incredible reality, and I'm so thrilled to be able to share Camp Maranatha with them.

Liz (Dobbs) Favela

In 1975, I joined my father ("Jeff" or Paul Jaffarian) for a whole week with some of my siblings. This was the first of four summers spent at Family Camp during my high school and college years. I remember my half-sister, "Katie" (actually Caitlin), being named "Short-Stop" by Mike Shea, for her baseball abilities; my half-brother, Rogers, being mistaken for a girl because of his long, curly hair; playing volleyball after snack bar with the camp staff; my brother Michael's "Awesome" sweatshirt; Reverend Aulis' Bible classes; having cabin mates like Jane Palmer (Jandayan), Claudia Smith (Jackson), Sally Anderson, and Cindy Chase (Moore). I met a lot of people who knew my parents (Jeff Jaffarian and Margaret Chambers Redfield) in college. People who knew my grandfathers (P.H. Jaffarian and Rolly Chambers) would fill me with stories of their early lives in ministry. Glendon Balser told me he lost his father (Buck) in the same car accident in which I lost my Grandfather Rolly Chambers and how he admired my grandmother (Ella Mae Chambers). A speaker named P.H. Augustine reminded me of my grandfather P.H. Jaffarian, both in initials and in size. I met people who knew my great-uncle (Ed Jaffarian) and heard stories of his part in the Southern California Advent Christian Conference and the beginnings of camp.

Family Camp

Our boys enjoyed Family Camp early in life. Timothy was seven months old his first week at camp and Isaac first came to Family Camp at three weeks of age.
Paula (Jaffarian) Shirley

When our daughter Katie (Cruce Kelly) was born, Family Camp became an annual event to which we looked forward every summer. Tom (my husband) was Family Camp Director in the summer of '84 when we had fun with a theme coinciding with the Olympic Games in Los Angeles. We had our own sporting competitions, and everyone went away with medals.
Sara (Summers) Cruce

Remembering . . . oh, nothin'

For those of you too old to remember, or those of you too young to know, Camp Maranatha used to serve as the scenic and unexpected earthly base for some of the most spectacular space launches of all time.

Undoubtedly, you've heard of Apollo 13. You've read the tales of John Glenn and Neil Armstrong. They deserve their place in history. But as far as heart-stopping adventure and thrills almost too much to bear goes, the daring exploits of unfamous Maranatha camper astronauts knows no comparison. I can only hope my erstwhile astronaut companions will forgive me for revealing so many secrets all these years later.

In short, camp was the home of two rather remarkable space ships that traversed the good old universe with a bold crew of good old children—perhaps too young and inexperienced to be afraid of the peril into which they placed themselves. Parents would have been alarmed, come running with outstretched arms, had they known that their

Mountain Top Experience

offspring, who *appeared* to be innocently playing upon those two enormous pine logs, long since felled and left to dry in twenty foot long sections outside the dining hall, were actually fighting alien menaces too horrible to even now recount.

The doubting scientists and engineers in the crowd may wish to know some of the specific design parameters of this ingenious craft. The end with the best knots and handholds and cut off limbs was the front. Everything had a purposeful reason to be there: knotholes, crevices, smooth places, and rough places were there to steer with and were battlements to man and places to secure oneself to when the inevitable trouble came. Boys and girls came and went in the game, according to their own muse. The captain could be anyone. The mission objective was variable as was its success. Sometimes we just had to crash and burn. Sometimes we did save the distant planet. One way or another we usually found *ourselves*. I mean, in the way that you find yourself when you lose yourself in your imagination.

The only real loser in these fanciful outer space voyages we took was time. Time seemed to get lost, to vanish under the swaying pines. And for the hearty few who kept "the story" going it could grow dark and chill, and the old bell atop the office would have long ago ceased clanging for dinner. Some adults might wonder where we were, and others would say, "They're still out there on that silly log." Finally, somebody's mom would pull a cardigan around her shoulders and come outside just far enough to scold in a shivering voice, "It's cold out here. Jimmy (the generic Jimmy), you and your friends come inside and get something to eat." It didn't apparently matter that we were in the fight of our lives, and the survival of mankind lay in the balance. It was time to eat.

Family Camp

And so into the humid warmth and the friendly, noisy clatter of the dining hall came a handful of intrepid adventurers fresh from interrupted glory. There was no fanfare. No thanks for the heroism. No John Glenn-type ticker-tape parade. But there was good food—and still warm. There was the smell of freshly brewed coffee and the sound of a million voices all talking at once. The gallant sojourners were coming back to earth and turning back into kids. We would balance our plate and cup and silverware, and a couple of rolls, find a place to sit, and become just ourselves again.

Maybe over in the corner someone was playing the piano. "Daisy, Daisy, give me your answer do . . ." sang the six or seven gathered around. Others warmed themselves by the fire. The kitchen staff ran the dishwasher and it whooshed and gurgled and hummed, and the stainless steel pots and pans sang their own songs, with help from the creaking and complaining of the swinging doors, and silverware trays crashing like cymbals in a Fourth of July parade as they dropped onto the counters. Campers and staffers alike, the combined energy of all these good old folk fairly pulsed like a heartbeat. Out of the din some well-meaning adult might lean closer and ask, "Say, what were you kids doing out on that log all this time." And in the time-honored tradition of kids and adults the answer could never be the truth—about the plot to rule the galaxy that we had just thwarted, or the ingenious solution conceived at the last minute to avert total disaster, or the gratitude of the people on that planet, the name of which no two kids pronounced the same way. Probably the only thing we could say was, "Oh, nothing," and that would have to suffice.

Sometimes a log is just a log. You might be sittin' there in the afternoon all by yourself. You find a sunny spot and

Mountain Top Experience

listen to the wind as it whistles past the hills and trees all around you. In the distance a diesel truck can be heard pulling an unwilling load up the mountain road. A confident, but wary, blue jay swoops down and sits momentarily by your side. Along might come that new kid you never met before. He'd say, "What ya doin'?" "Oh, nothin'." Soon, he's sittin' on the log, too, and somebody asks somebody where they come from, and a couple hours later they each got a new friend. From a ways off, a noise is heard. "Hey, isn't that the snack bar opening up?" "Yes, it is." And they wander down to see what everybody else is doing. Time passes.

And now time passes so quickly that it's been thirty years or more since those days passed for me. The logs are gone, hauled away. The carpenter ants ate a goodly part of them over generations of their insect lifetimes. Now only the memory of summers past and logs that could become anything you wanted them to be still exists.

We, who are lucky enough to still be alive and continue to love Camp Maranatha, appreciate that it is first and foremost a place for kids. Some of us were lucky enough to be the kids at camp. We have our memories, and they will stay with us. Now we owe it to *our* kids and the generations that follow to have the opportunity for such an experience. It may be a new friendship that lasts a lifetime, or inspiration that somehow couldn't come from down in the smoggy city, or a song echoing from Sunset Bowl, or a campfire, or even an old log. Whatever it might be, I will always believe that sometimes a log isn't just a log, and sometimes a camp isn't just a camp. It is much more.

Gene Crimi

Camp Couples

*It's bound to happen.
Take a hundred or so teenagers,
send them to camp for a week,
mix in a little star light,
fresh air,
fun times,
some serious times, too.
They're going to notice each other.
Some of them will really notice each other.
Lifetime friendships
are forged in such an environment
and sometimes,
lifetime partnerships as well.*

Mountain Top Experience

Before Maranatha, there was Camp Carlsbad. A few of us are still around who remember the campfires on the beach and evangelistic services in the big tent. It was the summer of 1935 when we met at the ten-day camp meeting. Betty was fourteen and Bob seventeen.

Bob and Betty Crimi
married 60 years

Phil proposed to me on the baseball diamond at Camp Maranatha under the stars. We have been married for twenty-seven years. I guess of all the memories, that one has to be the most special.

Phil and Debbie (Drew) Miller
married 27 years

I met my husband, Micah Gilbert, at Teen Camp in the summer of 1992. Even though both of us had been attending camp for as long as we could remember, we had never before met—probably because of the three-year age gap between us! That night, everyone was gathering in the bowl for the campfire, and I was heading back to my cabin to get a sweatshirt. Micah happened to walk by and he gave me one of his, since his cabin was right by the bowl and mine was "way out in the baseball field." I thought Micah was a nice guy, and I promised to write to him during the upcoming year. But I didn't end up sending him any letters.

The following summer, I was anxious to get back to camp. I had just finished my first year of high school and had broken up with my first real boyfriend the day before I left to be a counselor at Kids Kamp. The last thing I was interested in was boys. I was excited about spending time at Kid's Kamp and Teen Camp to get refocused on God. When I returned to Maranatha for Teen Camp, I was very

Camp Couples

surprised to see Micah sitting on a bench. He said "Hi" and apologized that he couldn't remember my name. During the week, we got to know each other better and developed a mutual interest. Despite Sarah Paulson (Tate)'s insistence that Micah and I were going to get married, I was sure that we wouldn't be seeing much of each other since we lived 120 miles apart. Besides, I was only fifteen, and he was eighteen.

But Micah and I did see each other, and things got pretty serious. In fact, in July of 1996, Micah proposed to me, and we were married at the First Advent Christian Church of Tustin on July 18, 1998. We have now been happily married for four years. We live in Denver and have started a family. I do hope that someday our children will be able to attend camps at Camp Maranatha. They will definitely be familiar with the place that has played such an important role in their parents' lives. Micah and I have been blessed with wonderful friends, great memories, meeting each other, and a strong foundation for our faith—all in thanks to this fantastic retreat in the mountains and the wonderful people who are always there.

Micah and Christina (Parker) Gilbert
married four years

Carol Aulis Muska remembers decorating the honeymoon cabin at Kids Kamp for Chief Honey and Chief Moon:
"What other couple would choose to spend their honeymoon at camp?"
Chief Honey and Chief Moon are perhaps better known as:

Dick and Nancy (Crimi) Beggs
married 39 years

Mountain Top Experience

I met my future husband at Family Camp. The first two years I went, Keith was on summer staff. He asked for my address after my second summer. We exchanged a few letters, then the writing would stop until the next year when we would see each other again at Family Camp. Those years of getting acquainted involved volleyball games, watching staff guys work at rebuilding the bowl, sitting next to each other in services and fire circles, staying up until 2:00 A.M. talking while watching shooting stars from the upper end girls bathroom steps (who ever thought bathroom steps could hold memories!). My life in Oregon and Keith's college life took us different directions for years even though we still wrote periodically.

During the early '80s, I was brought back to camp again on a regular basis. This time, it was more of a courtship. We had long talks in the car while going to and from camp, collected rocks to build a fountain, collected more rocks to build dams in the gully, watched block upon block being laid to make the dam taller, used a shovel to fill in dirt behind the dam, checked out how the dam broke and rebuilt it (with Dave Crimi as the "foreman," of course). These times together did eventually lead to marriage. But even after marriage, camp continued to be an integral part of our lives.

Keith and Paula Shirley
married 20 years

The first year I worked on camp staff, in 1959, I met my husband, Keith Froehlich. Juanita Hunt, who was the camp director with her husband, Errol, introduced Keith and me at the Presbyterian Church. She said, "If my girls don't get him, I'm going to get him for you!" We started writing to each other and ended up married two years later in August 1961.

Camp Couples

We lived at the camp for the summer after we got married (thanks to Juanita and Errol), because Keith worked for the State Forest Service in Idyllwild. Then we traveled to Evanston, Illinois, for Keith to attend Garrett Theological Seminary. Camp Maranatha "gave" me a minister to marry (and a great guy too!).
Keith and Bonnie (Pitts) Froehlich
married 40 years

I think it's impossible to put our camp life into one experience. One thing is for sure as we look back over the years . . . God is awesome. He took two totally separate people from two totally different situations and brought us together at exactly the perfect time. Our marriage is full of Camp Maranatha history. The fun, the work, the relationships, and, most important, the Lord. We love sharing our stories with our six kids. We both accepted the Lord at Camp Maranatha years ago and our lives have not been the same.

Even though it's difficult to stay in touch, everyone we ever worked with at camp holds a special place in our hearts.
Scott and Holly (Plummer) McCaghren
married ten years

My husband, Pete Mergens, and I met at Camp Maranatha as a result of the wiles of our mutual friend, Darlene Rigney. Pete and I had met briefly at a young adult retreat in March of 1990, when my sister Elise and I were brushing snow off his car and he emphatically told us to stop, because he didn't want us to scratch the paint! That was pretty much the end of our first meeting.

In August of that same year, Darlene called me toward the end of the week of Teen Camp to ask if I would help her out by coming up to finish the week for one of her counselors who had gotten sick. I grudgingly said yes (I had other

Mountain Top Experience

plans) and went up to help her out. She said that I could catch a ride up with Dave Crimi, but that she didn't know how I would get home. I was a little hesitant to go up not knowing how I was going to get home, but I went anyway.

Darlene knew full well how she was planning on getting me home. She was going to ask her friend Pete to give me a ride home, since we both lived in San Diego. So, at the "last minute," I caught a ride with Pete and we instantly hit it off and talked all the way home. However, nothing came of it at that point.

In September, Darlene asked me to go to the young adult retreat. I said I didn't have any money and that I didn't think I would be going. She tried to entice me and said that she would be going and that our friend Lisa (Crist) would be there . . . and, oh yes, she mentioned that Pete would be going, too. I responded that I was not interested because he already had a girlfriend (who lived in Canada) and that I was not really looking for anyone. (I had just come out of a long relationship that was hurtful and had sworn off men.) She insisted that he was going to break up with her and that all would be okay. So, once again, she arranged for Pete to pick me up and give me a ride to camp. I was living with my good friend Cary (Beggs) Bursvold at the time.

I remember that weekend well: playing cards late at night in the dining hall, endless football games, sitting around the fire at the bowl while Dave Tapley and Pete played guitar and Lisa and I sang. I remember that Pete leaned against me that night and I was so nervous and a little freaked out! I also remember that he asked to borrow a blanket the first night because he had forgotten to bring one, and I thought he was a little irresponsible (as well as uptight about his car!).

That was the beginning of the beginning for Pete and me. I discovered he is not uptight about his car, and he is

Camp Couples

anything but irresponsible! We have been very happy together for eleven years now and have two beautiful little girls God has given us. Those memories of camp are so precious to me, and those times with Darlene, also. Camp Maranatha is a place that has served to bring us together in the Lord, and keep us together in the Lord. We have shared being counselors at teen retreats as well as leading music. Little did I know as a child, playing with Cary at camp summer after summer, that God was preparing me for Pete and that our relationship would develop at that very same place. Thank you, Darlene!

Pete and Jane (Gransee) Mergens
married eleven years

Other Camp Couples include:

Mike and Anna (McGath) Tapley *married ten years*—their courtship started at camp.

Mark and Sherry (Foutz) Wickens *married twenty-one years*—their courtship started at camp when they worked on staff together.

Denny and Shannon (Wickens) Lazar *married four years*—They had a "romantic honeymoon" in the Log House with their sons, Johnathan and Michael, and dog, Duchess, along for the fun.

Christopher and Katherine (Fleming) Blakely *married four years*—their wedding ceremony was performed at Camp Maranatha.

Josh and Sarah (Paulson) Tate *married one year*—they met as summer staffers in 1994 and had their wedding ceremony performed at Camp Maranatha in June of 2001.

Syed and Amber (Quintana) Anis *married four years*—their wedding ceremony was performed at Camp Maranatha.

People We Recall

*There is something unique about the relationships
formed in camping.
Something about sharing meals,
classes,
recreation,
prayer,
and sleeping quarters
binds us more deeply and quickly
than in the more frequent
but less constant contact
we have with our
neighbors,
co-workers,
fellow students,
and Sunday school classmates.
Even though many of our camp relationships live only
for a week or weekend,
they remain with us in an inscrutable way.*

Mountain Top Experience

It follows that a book about camp experiences will be filled with names—
Names of the people who live on in camp memories.
Some of those mentioned may never have even been to Camp Maranatha,
yet they contributed, in some way,
to a camper's journey.
Few who read this will recognize every name,
but they are all important.
Each one,
as well as many others who live on in camp stories
that never made it onto paper,
is a part of the human tapestry of Camp Maranatha.
Read and remember the people you met
in your own camp journey.

People We Recall

It is amazing to me how clearly r
you despite thirty-three years of tir
my eyes and see the camp and brir
have not seen since that encounter.
them by name, and their faces are locked in
even now.

Today, no longer living in California, the majority of the people with whom I do stay in contact are friends made during my camping experience, whether as a camper, counselor, or staff member. I may never see these friends again this side of heaven, but I know we'll have a great reunion one day.

Debbie (Peckens) Hammond

My mother first went to camp at Carlsbad. One of her friends was Andy Smith. (After I was born, some people thought I was related to Andy because of my red hair!) My parents, Charles and Norma (Mansfield) Howard, hailed from opposite ends of the country, but they met and married at Aurora College. I was born in 1948, and about a year later we moved to California and attended the Advent Christian Church in Colton. I remember going to church with the Barths, Bowdens, and Buckleys. I remember the Foxs and Scotts visiting and sharing their music with us and Mrs. Bowden drawing chalk pictures during the sermon. She drew the large picture of Jesus ascending into Heaven in the clouds. That picture was in the Colton church until it was torn down. The last I knew, it was in the Tustin church over the baptistry. I love that picture, partly because I saw it so much while I was a child.

Cindy (Howard) Bailey

Mountain Top Experience

Some of my most emotional experiences at Camp Maranatha have come when it was time to leave. Either after a camp or a whole summer, leaving has always been difficult for me, because it has always meant leaving friends. Friends we have known long or just come to know. Friends we have learned to love.

I remember on one occasion it was time to go and I was crying my head off. My mom came to pick me up really early because a close relative was getting married on that day. But Darlene Rigney offered to drive me home. I was the happiest guy in the world because of the gift of a few extra hours at Camp Maranatha.

In December of 2000, I brought my wife and kids up to visit Camp Maranatha for a few days. Again, leaving was hard, but not as hard, because my destination was to see good friends that I had grown up with at camp. We hadn't seen each other in many years. Anyhow, within fifteen minutes of our arrival at Mike and Anna Tapley's house, we were sitting out on their terrace reminiscing about our "mountain top experiences." We stayed for two days and talked about a lot of other things, things that I vaguely remember, but the terrace conversation will not be forgotten!!!

Robert Underwood

I have many memories of my cousins Scott (Summers) and Katie (Cruce Kelly). We would stay up for hours just talking about anything and everything. I remember the way Chris (Slater), Mike (Slusser) and Devin (Parker) would make us all laugh until we couldn't feel our faces and our sides hurt. I especially remember the songs Dave Tapley would sing with his guitar and the silly ones he would make up. I was young, and that impressed me. I ended up marry-

People We Recall

ing a songwriter. I don't know if that had something to do with it.

Gwen (Koehler) Marron

Pastor Phil Shuman was always coming up with some witticism. Once, at snow camp, he had all of us campers shout out "BANANAS!" then told us what a good "bunch" we were.

I remember Jack(ie) Carlton, a fellow camper my age, and his older brother, Rusty, Nathan Sanderson (from my church), and Jamie Jackson, who was the perennial favorite to receive the tribal chief's beaded necklace. He had an older sister (Liz), Chief Red Fox, who was a counselor. There was Pastor Phil's son, Mark. Then there was Todd Bisgard, David Yost, Becky Tyler, Lori Miller, and so many more that my mind refuses to allow me to recall.

Kevin Castleman

There is one particular place at Camp Maranatha that holds a very special meaning for me. During the summer or winter months, or whenever I visit with friends at Camp Maranatha, I always try to spend as much time as I can in the Gazebo. It is there that the wonderful memories of Darlene Rigney return to my mind. This small structure, erected in her memory, reminds me of her love, kindness, and the unique friendship we shared. Spending time alone in the Gazebo always makes me feel like Darlene's spirit surrounds me with a special kind of peace.

Even though Darlene and I were very close as friends and as sisters in Christ, I also felt close to Darlene as if we were born sisters when we took our frequent trips to *Subway* for lunch or to *7-11* for a Big Gulp. I always enjoyed and treasured the times and opportunities we shared by

Mountain Top Experience

just being together as friends. I would often go to Bible study with Darlene when it was held at other church people's houses, and being a part of the "MIX" group (a musical group of young adults from North Park Community Church) when we would go to sing songs to elderly church members in convalescent homes. I also remember going to San Diego Padres baseball games with Darlene. I enjoyed the gentle rivalry and joking with each other when the Los Angeles team came to town. Darlene always cheered for the Dodgers while I remained true to the Padres.

It is true that Darlene Rigney is gone from our midst now, but in a way she is still with us. Her memory lives on in my heart and in the hearts of so many others she touched with her generosity and friendship. In the silent moments of the Gazebo at Camp Maranatha, I sense that her spirit still remains, in some special way, here in this spot that honors her name.

I still love and miss Darlene so very much, even though I know I'll see her again someday. I'm so glad I have this special place to go where I can reflect on the times we shared and enjoy the gentle peace of the God she loved and served.

Anna Mae Gardner

Our family's connection with the camp has been close over the years. All three kids attended Kids Kamp. Betty served as crafts instructor for about thirty years and as a Teen Camp counselor. Son David gave almost ten years of his young life helping Errol develop many of the facilities we enjoy today. Now, Nancy and Dick are completing thirty years of camp management. Our grandchildren (Jody, Cary, and Kevin) and now great-grandchildren (Brian and Ashly Reeves) have been on the camp summer staff.

Bob and Betty Crimi

People We Recall

Spending time up at Camp Maranatha has provided me with my dearest and closest friends, like Ben Gama, Gabe Gama, Sarah Paulson (Tate), James Almon, and, of course, Darlene Rigney.

Christina (Parker) Gilbert

Being a third-generation camper (my grandmother, Lillian Koehler, loved to tell us about Carlsbad) I always felt at home at Camp Maranatha. Even when I visited a couple years ago while I was on vacation, it was comfortable to be there.

Sheldon Koehler

During college, camps eluded me due to studies, and I did not know of any camps for the college ages. I deeply missed church camps. Otis and I married about a year after college and both of us were caught up in careers when Camp Maranatha entered our lives for a short period of time.

After seven years of marriage, our beloved son was born. He was the most precious thing on earth, and we could not get enough of him. Everywhere we went, Charles went. We were attending a church in LaVerne that had wonderful people, and we were happy there. We had a neighbor on the block, a heavy-set woman with four sons, who attended services in this cracker-box shaped building called Bonita Avenue Church and kept inviting us to attend. We said no thank you, we were attending a good, Bible-teaching church.

Our church was constructing a new building with Sunday school rooms and a new nursery begging to be filled with children. But our son was quiet during church and we stayed in the back row so we wouldn't bother anyone. Finally, a younger mother with an older hyperactive daughter who gloried in the nursery said, "My pet peeve is people who don't put their children in the nursery, because I do."

Mountain Top Experience

I thought to myself that it was possible she put her daughter in the nursery because she needed the break. I decided that if my child wasn't welcome in the service, then neither were we.

We remembered Dorothy Luton's invitation, so we started attending Bonita Avenue Church. It was love at first sight. I could not believe how much the inside of the building resembled my childhood church. And the people were great! Oh, yes, I did lose my son on Sunday mornings. Bunny Berdeen, Ruth Titus, and Dorothy Luton took turns holding the "baby" so the parents could enjoy the service. They sat beside us and held him. I often wondered, *did they flip a coin to see who got to hold him each Sunday?*

Jeannie Davis

If you were not at the camp about thirty or so years ago, you are not going to know who I am. Don't try to figure me out. Dick and Nancy will know me, as will Dave Crimi. I was on camp staff with Chris Blakely, Debbie Clawitter, Debbie Peckens (Hammond), "Chicken" (Kathy Hahn Bottom), Jamie, and I will think of the rest in a minute. I was from the Tustin church. Ah, Dwight Shirley and Kris Combs (Snyder) were two other persons. I went to Aurora College in 1972 with Dwight, Chris B., and Debbie Peckens. In my adult life I became a law enforcement officer with the City of Tustin. I now live in the "Panhandle" of North Idaho, in the Coeur d' Alene area. Had enough?

Does Al March ring a bell? Yes? No? Maybe? I still have contact via the internet with Debbie Peckens a.k.a. Hammond. My sister, Paula, came up to camp many times. Last hint. This was back in the Mike Shea times (God rest his soul). Does the name "Beanie" ring a bell with anyone? If not, then you are a lot older than you are admitting to, and your memory is usually the first thing to go :-).

Al "Beanie" March

People We Recall

It wasn't until many years after Gene Crimi and I impressed each other at Kids Kamp by boasting of our prestigious relatives that I learned Gene's dad (Bob Crimi) and his uncle (Jim Crimi) had grown up with my dad and my uncles and attended the Advent Christian Church Camp in Carlsbad and had all gone to the famous Aurora college together. I didn't know that Gene's family and my family had connections that went back generations, back to our great-grandparents on both sides, or rather all sides—it gets a little confusing. And just as I didn't know anything then about our family bonds, I had no way of knowing that Gene and I would ride the train back to Aurora to attend the same college. Or that his dad and mom and his brother David and sister Nancy and their cousins would be my friends and loved ones for the rest of my life.

Because we didn't have an Advent Christian Church near where I lived, Camp Maranatha was really the only place where I could discover these friendships that were new to me, but had actually begun years before I was born by people I would never know. So while I have countless memories of camp, some of which I suspect did actually happen, it's the people who made those memories possible that I cherish. I may be able to make up memories, but I can't make up people. Well, actually, I can, but for our purposes here let's just pretend I can't.

Jamo Jackson

When Darlene (Rigney) got sick and was in the hospital, I wanted to see her. I prayed and prayed that she would be all right for us. I thought she might not be okay, so instead I prayed to send a message to her. "Please, God, let her know how much I love and miss her and I am sorry I couldn't be there." I woke up some time in the early morning from a dream in which the teens and counselors were

Mountain Top Experience

at camp in the Two-Story. I came in the front door. Darlene came over to me, took my hand and said, "I am alright." At that moment, I felt such an overwhelming feeling of joy and sadness. I tried to stop her, but I couldn't speak. Then I woke up and told my husband Erik. The telephone rang early the next morning and I knew exactly what we would be told. I learned that God can do things that you think are impossible so believe and be patient. After Darlene left us it was apparent that she handled so much. We all tried to continue her work, as we felt this would be like keeping a part of Darlene alive.

Denise Stiers

Nestled in God's high country (Idyllwild, California), is a Christian-based camp named Camp Maranatha, managed by God's chosen couple, a couple I came to know well.

When searching my mind and heart for a way to illustrate Dick and Nancy Beggs' character, values, and relationship with me, my family, and our community, I found the perfect description in the Bible. "But the fruit of the Spirit is love, joy, peace, patience, kindness, goodness, faithfulness, gentleness, and self-control. Against such things there is no law" (Galatians 5:22–23).

Truly, we will know God's people when we see the love, joy, peace, patience, kindness, goodness, faithfulness, gentleness, and self-control of God in them. This I found in Dick and Nancy Beggs. It is evident that Dick and Nancy were given a heart to be a part of Christian camping. God equipped them with the authority and wisdom to manage Camp Maranatha; this I know first hand.

From 1981 through 1992, my family was blessed by Dick and Nancy and witnessed God's outstretched hand of charity, encouragement, compassion, and love through them. Over and over, my young and financially struggling

People We Recall

family was blessed by our connection to the camp and Dick and Nancy. There were times when I worked side by side with this couple. I remember watching them manage the staff as I believed God would. And to the camp visitors, they were true servants.

We moved from Idyllwild to Bend, Oregon, in 1992. But my heart knows full well the great testimony that Dick and Nancy shall *always* be to me and my family. I believe a multitude of witnesses have known, and will continue to know them as pillars in the Christian camp experience and in their community.

When one meets people who really know the Lord, it is life changing for that moment and possibly forever. This is my tribute to an awesome man and woman of God, faithful in all that He asked of them.

Saundra Caron (Reynolds)

What Camp Maranatha means to me is *family*, from remembering the blessing of my heritage, to raising my own family here on the grounds. My initial visit to camp was in 1972 when the Advent Christian General Conference had their meeting in Orange County. I came to California with my Jaffarian grandparents (P.H. and Flo), visited my father ("Jeff" or Paul Jaffarian), and my uncle and aunt, John and Carol Palmer. The Palmers brought me to Idyllwild to see the camp during Family Camp. I only remember the pool, parking lot, and playing with my Palmer cousins.

The 90s brought us to camp to live as a family. Keith had taken the job as facility manager to work alongside the Beggs. Timothy was four and Isaac was two. Larissa was born in 1991. So camp has allowed Keith and me to see our children grow up. Memories are hikes, both on the grounds and off, learning to ride bikes and unicycles and making coasters, Sunday afternoon roller hockey games, volleyball

Mountain Top Experience

games, swimming, sledding, working, and sharing. Family times with extended family visiting too. During these years we have gained wonderful memories with a staff family of teenagers. There are staff guy stories and dog stories, many volleyball games, movies, adventures off the hill, and enjoying having nieces and nephews (Jeremy Redfield, David Shirley, Grant, Tara, and Calvin Jaffarian) join us on staff for the summer. Now our family includes volunteers who share meals with us, work alongside Keith, and play card games after the work is done.

The common bond of Christ allows these family memories to be a part of Camp Maranatha. There is family history here, family memories, and family growth. The investment of time and lives into this camp has made Maranatha a place to come together and grow.

Paula (Jaffarian) Shirley

Watching Dick, Nancy, staff and volunteers was a real blessing to me. Even the presence of "Moose," "Duke," and "Dolly," the camp dogs, was part of the spirit of Camp Maranatha. An additional blessing of being on site was developing relationships with Kevin (Beggs), Joe, Jody, Ashly, and Brian (Reeves). I am pleased, too, that through the years we have been able to nurture these relationships and share in their lives.

Ralph Reid

Camp Maranatha was a wonderful place to establish relationships with people of all ages and generations. Christian role models and Christian friendships established there are still treasured.

Carol (Aulis) Muska

People We Recall

My first camp counselor was Pat Eng. She called herself Grandma Oobie, and filled the void of mother with her tender care and thoughtfulness.

Liz (Dobbs) Favela

I've only been on staff for two years, but I know there will be many more to come. I'm not sure what it is that makes me feel the way I do when I'm at Camp Maranatha, but what I do know is that I want camp to be part of me for the rest of my life. For as long as I can remember (not so long—I'm only sixteen) camp was one thing I would look forward to year round. My dad (Chuck) went as a kid, my grandma (Carol) lived there as a young adult, and my great-grandparents (Erroll and Juanita Hunt) had the blessing of living there for over twenty years as Camp Maranatha's first managers.

Melissa Matthews

I have very fond memories of all the years I worked at Camp Maranatha and have a lot of respect and admiration for all the Hunts put up with from some of the earlier staff days. We had a lot of fun, did a lot of work, and learned many things that are still with me and helping me today. Through all my years of work and even to the present time, Errol Hunt is the best boss I have ever worked for, and I want to thank him for the many opportunities of learning he has given me. Never once did I see Errol alarmed or excited about any incident that happened at the camp. Believe me, there were plenty of "incidents" while I was there.

If Juanita Hunt has any gray hair, I know the boys staff had to be responsible for some of it. At one camp, we heard the girls (campers) were going to raid the kitchen one evening and we decided that we would give them a big surprise. Some of us took #10 cans and filled them with water

Mountain Top Experience

and hid under the tables. When the girls came in, we threw the water on them with the cans making all kinds of noise as they hit the floor. With all this splashing, banging, and screaming going on, Juanita woke up and we could see her coming down the walk. I don't think the girls saw her, but we took off out the back doors and into our cabin. The girls not only had a surprise from us, but they also had to deal with Juanita.

After she left the cafeteria, Juanita came directly to our cabin. Not a sound did we make. She pounded on the door and said, "I know you boys are in there," but not a sound did we make. Juanita did this several times and then went back home. I just want you to know, Juanita, we were in there, but we sure were not going to make a sound. You understand, I'm sure, we couldn't let the girls raid the kitchen without doing something about it.

Then there was the time we sent Barry Tate through the big dishwasher. We talked Barry into doing this and told him if he ran out of air halfway through to be sure to yell real loud and we would turn it off. We filled it with warm water, laid Barry on about four trays, and sent him through. Everything worked out and Barry came out nice and clean. For about three days after that, I ate off of paper plates until I felt the dishwasher was nice and clean. That was probably the best bath Barry had all that summer. No offense, Barry!

Speaking of Barry, did you ever hear about Barry and the yellow jackets? We had a problem with yellow jackets by the shuffleboard court (at that time located behind the craft building) and one of the campers asked Barry to do something about it. Barry did solve the problem for awhile, but it came right back at him. He took a stick and put it in the yellow jacket hole so they would not come out. That

People We Recall

was fine until later that evening when he removed the stick and all the yellow jackets came swarming out after him. He started yelling and running with yellow jackets stinging and chasing him. Paul McIver was laughing so hard he couldn't move. As Barry ran past him, I think some of the yellow jackets stung Paul and got him up and running. I was up in the hills behind the A-Frame and could hear the commotion from there. One thing about Camp Maranatha, it gave us all a chance to learn what *not* to do.

Speaking of what *not* to do, the next story is a good example of something not to pass on to the present-day staff. We used to have these heavy china dishes. When you had a rack full of them it was quite heavy and at times they did break, but it seemed our inventory of dishes that summer never got very low. There was a reason for this. Across the hill there was either a Boy Scout or Girl Scout camp that was not in use at the time. Their chinaware was about the same as Camp Maranatha's and somehow made its way to our kitchen. I was not involved with this transaction, and out of staff loyalty, refuse to incriminate anyone, but it did take place. We never told anyone about this, but knowing Errol he probably heard about it later and kept it quiet.

Ken Steinseifer

Camp is where I met one of my dearest friends, Carolyn (Schenk) Gillogly. As prayer partners at Teen Camp in 1988,* we discovered the importance of accountability and Christian friendship. Together at camp we first experienced the transforming power of prayer and encouraged each other to live out our daily commitment to Christ back home, in my case "off the mountain" (Carolyn lived in Idyllwild). That divinely appointed friendship changed my life forever, and we still pray for each other across thousands of miles,

Mountain Top Experience

thanks to our meeting at Camp Maranatha so many years ago.

Katie (Cruce) Kelly

*Editors note: For more on this story, read Carolyn's entry in the Teen Camp section.

I have many happy memories of Camp Maranatha. Camp is where I met some of my closest friends. Or maybe I should say it is where a bunch of giggly Idyllwild girls got to spend some great times together. I also met many wonderful people from all walks of life. What a blessing it was to have such a quality Christian camp right in my hometown. Thank you Dick and Nancy for all your hard work and dedication. Your reward in heaven will be great, I'm sure. Thanks, Jody, for being my special friend. God used you and your family to bless my life in many ways. May God bless you!

Jeanette (Schenk) Henneberry

Phil Shuman directed most of the teen camps and retreats during my growing-up years at Camp Maranatha. Some of us, at the time, mistreated Phil and failed to appreciate the spiritual role he was playing in our lives. Now that he's no longer alive for me to tell, I've come to thank God for him and to love him.

Two things stand out about a particular snow retreat. Just outside the door at the far end of the dining hall, I watched him split a log for that night's fire-side service. Using a sledge hammer, it took him at least three, maybe four, wedges to do the job. Then, by the firelight, he taught us a chorus in his rough, vibrant voice, the words of which have stayed with me all these years: "Lord of all, or not Lord at all. Christ must be Lord of all."

Barry Joe Tate

People We Recall

Many of my family members have a connection with Camp Maranatha. My grandparents (Ray and Jennie Mills) went to camp there and I think my Grandma Jennie used to go with my dad, Earl Wright, and uncles, and aunt when they were kids. When my dad worked on staff as a teenager, he helped lay the foundation of the old Tabernacle. His initials may still be found there. My brother, David Wright, also worked on summer staff.

Candee (Wright) Schreiner

I grew up in Idyllwild, so Camp Maranatha was just around the corner from where I lived. I shared a cabin with the same group of girls for several years in a row: Katie Cruce, Misty Wilson, Erin Calkins, Amy Gustafson (Hagin), Amy Gosnell, Lynn Childress, and Brandi Harris. I recall some intense times of arguing and some equally intense times of making up.

I remember a counselor named Mike Tapley who was so good to us kids and had such a heart for the Lord. He was always available and willingly took part in all the games we played. The most fun was the all-out water balloon war. There was not a dry article of clothing after that game! I also remember a dear counselor by the name of Darlene Rigney. She was wonderful. She was so patient with us even though we gave her so much trouble, and she kept coming back year after year! She is with the Lord now, but her Christ-like character and example have impacted many lives. I'm convinced she must have known what storing her treasure in heaven was all about.

I also remember a person who was too often taken for granted. Nancy Beggs faithfully provided meals for us grateful kids, or was that *ungrateful* kids? I guess it depended on what was on the menu!

Mountain Top Experience

I remember one summer when Dick Beggs planted grass and he was determined no one would step on it. Try keeping a hundred teenagers off brand new grass, it's no easy chore, but Dick did a great job! He was a focused man and he was set on growing grass that summer, even though few in Idyllwild have succeeded. (We still stepped on it when he wasn't looking.)

I simply can't forget all the laughing I did at camp, thanks to friends like Scott Summers, Michael Slusser, Erin Calkins, and Kim Tapley. I still cherish their sense of humor. I have to add that two of my dearest friends to this day are girls I shared a cabin with—Katie Cruce and Misty Wilson (now Katie Kelly and Misty McKinley). I love you guys!

Carolyn (Schenk) Gillogly

Teen Camp

Don't let anyone look down on you because you are young, but set an example for the believers in speech, in life, in love, in faith and in purity.
1 Timothy 4:12

Mountain Top Experience

For decades, the Advent Christian Conference of Southern California has been striving to reach teens with the gospel of Jesus Christ through its yearly Teen Camp and bi-yearly retreats at Camp Maranatha. I first attended Teen Camp around age thirteen. Little did I know at that young, spry age the significance Camp Maranatha would have in my life throughout the years to come. At teen camps and retreats, I have filled many shoes from camper to director. Over the years, I've had the privilege of directing camps with Martha (Gransee) Fernandez, Cary (Beggs) Bursvold, Darlene Rigney, Ron Knapp, Elise (Gransee) Finney, and, most recently, my wife Jody. (Since other directors would come and go, I thought I should marry one to keep her around. Jody and I have now directed teen camps and retreats for five years.) Each role I've filled, no matter how big or small, has played its part in shaping me into the man God created me to be. I thank the Lord for making those opportunities available to me through Camp Maranatha.

My life is just one of many that has been changed. Through Camp Maranatha, the Advent Christian Conference of Southern California has ministered to hundreds of teens. I have seen Teen Camp evolve over the years to meet the needs of new generations, but the main purpose has remained: to reach young people with the life-changing love of Jesus Christ. It has been an awesome blessing to watch God change lives! Many young people are drawn back to Camp Maranatha (as I was) year after year to a familiar safe place where they will be loved and where they will make relationships that last a lifetime. It is a privilege to witness these teens as they grow in the Lord. They may come back for the fun, games, and friendships, but what really draws them is the unconditional love of the heavenly Father. At Teen Camp, they experience it again and again through a

Teen Camp

speaker, a hug, a shoulder to cry on, or a counselor who listens. It is this unconditional love that teens will always be searching for, and it is this unconditional love that we want Teen Camp to always provide.

Many have returned wanting to give back to the Lord and others what they have been given. Many come back to Camp Maranatha as counselor, speaker, or director. I am confident they will be as blessed as I have been.

Dave Crimi

At Teen Camp, the light we saw shining through our window wasn't Phil Shuman's flashlight, but the sun rising—we'd talked all night! I remember sleeping with our makeup at snow retreat, so it wouldn't freeze . . . Bette Beauchamp refusing to go to breakfast 'til her eyelashes were curled . . . being Youth Fellowship President when the basketball court *finally* got built (guess it took a woman to get things done!) . . . the friendships we made . . . the memories we keep . . . they are all precious and with me always. I thank God that we had Camp Maranatha as such a focal point in our lives.

Leslie (McIver) Hutchins

It seems as though Camp Maranatha has always been a part of me, yet my first experience there was as a camper at "Western Adven-Chur" the summer of 1968. I was fifteen years old and would be entering high school in September. I went to camp at the invitation of good school friends, Diane Vadman and Shirley Anderson. I wore a Star of David, following the Jewish side of my heritage, but really did not believe in anything. A counselor, Lynn Parker, listened to my statements of disbelief and encouraged me to read the Bible, pray, and seek God. I accepted Christ as my personal Lord and Savior the last night of camp and left the mountain as a new creature in Christ.

Mountain Top Experience

During the week of Teen Camp, we played a game called Pony Express. While participating in a wheelbarrow race, I took my shoes off. When I returned "to whence I left them (near the flag pole)," they were gone. Little did I know that Lynn Parker had turned them in to lost and found. I soon learned that in order to retrieve items from lost and found, you had to stand in front of everyone in the dining hall and sing a song, dance, recite a poem, or do something to earn the item back! I wrote a poem about losing my shoes and read it out loud at dinner. I was inwardly dying of embarrassment and outwardly flaming red. Here is the poem:

> Today at camp we played a game
> And in my opinion it was insane
> While getting ready I laid down my shoes
> To find out later my shoes I did lose
> When they were found Uncle Phil said, "Whose?"
> So now Uncle Phil may I please have my shoes?
> **Debbie (Peckens) Hammond**

Soon after my first time at Family Camp, I was asked to be a teen counselor. It was great to experience some of the things I missed as a teenager. As a counselor I came to realize the things I had gone through as a teen myself could help me to relate to the campers.

Teen camp has been the location of many memorable occasions like the counselor hunts. Chris Blakely has always hidden in a place where even the other counselors could not find him. My favorite hiding place was the trash can. With the trash all on top of me, even a dirty can would suffice. I finally gave it up because my knees wouldn't let me go there again. Darlene was always the person targeted for teen terrorism. Her poor Hyundai had anything possible done to it. If they could have put it on the roof of the

Teen Camp

ice-cream parlor they would have. She knew it was coming, and was always a good sport, anyway.

One experience I remember so well from Teen Camp was the overnight hike to the top of San Jacinto. There were about thirty people when we started out. The clouds appeared ominous in the sky, but no sign of rain. We took plastic bags just in case, as most of us had not brought rain gear. It started raining approximately four hours into the hike and we were not quite halfway at this point. By the time we reached the upper camp we were entirely soaked. It had stopped raining for a little while, but we were very hungry and were having trouble lighting the stove. So we improvised with a can opener and several cans of Spaghettios. (I was sick of Spaghettios after that.) The rain resumed after dinner so we hurried to a nearby ranger tent. My husband and I got to lay down on the cots and finally got warm and dry. Approximately an hour later the kids came filing in with their wet clothes and wet sleeping bags. This tent was only designed to sleep five or six people and, after about an hour, we had the whole bunch in there. Somehow, I got up and lost my place and that left me with standing room only. I was exhausted, so I piled up the wet sleeping bags outside the door and got under them. The good part about that was I didn't have anyone's feet in my face or heads on my stomach. I think I made out better than the rest. We got up at daylight and slowly made our way to the top of the mountain, freezing, wet, and tired. This experience blessed us with closeness, prayer, new and lasting friendships, and a beautiful next day on the mountain—a once in a lifetime experience.

I remember the good times and the bad Camp Maranatha provided me. Yes, believe it or not, there were bad times, but those bad times taught me and brought me closer to God. Sometimes we only learn through adversity, because

Mountain Top Experience

we humans are stubborn. There are many examples of this in the Bible. We need to know this and strive to do better next time. On a beautiful August afternoon in 1990, a boy named Jon Sanderson fell to his death off of Suicide Rock. He was under the care of Rod (Sherry), Lisa (Sherry), Ron (Knapp) and myself. He had gone too far and slipped. We sent the other campers back and waited patiently for help to arrive. We had hours to reflect on what had happened, how we were responsible somehow, hoping he was still alive, trying desperately to get down to him, wishing to never hear or see the reaction of his mother. As a mother, I would be devastated, and I could only imagine how Jon's mother would feel. I was severely depressed and all I could do was cry. I didn't want anything to do with anybody. I had anxiety attacks and I simply fell into a hole. The only people who knew how I felt were Ron, Rod and Lisa. What did I learn? That God never goes away, but we do! Sometimes what we want and what we get are two different things. I wanted so much to give Jon back to his mother, but deep down, no matter how I prayed, I knew I could not.

Denise Stiers

My standout Teen Camp memories include:
Moonlight hikes and swims; skits - especially when we would lip sync to Bill Cosby recordings by "Pasadena Gang" (I *think* they were Bill Cosby - my memory is lapsing. Maybe Smothers Brothers?). "Borrowing" the donkey from the stables next door and tying it to "Uncle Phil" Shuman's cabin. Campfires.

Carol (Aulis) Muska

As a camper, I recall making radio shows, writing camp newspapers, pony express relay races, crafts, my attempts at sports activities, and talent shows. Lisa Sherry taught me

Teen Camp

volley ball, thus inspiring Chris Slater and Mike Slusser to nickname me Chief Tipping Teepee. One summer my sister Beth was tied to a bunk, hauled across camp, and placed under the boys' shower, bunk and all.

The most spectacular talent show of all was when the twelfth-grade boys, the cabin of the 80s, stole Brad Rigney's sleeping bag and made him earn it back by dressing up in various female costumes and posing at various points around the camp. The coupe d'etat was the slide presentation in the talent show at the end of the week, featuring "Bo Rigney—A Negative 10."

As a counselor for the first time, I was completing the cabin inspection of the girls' cabins. I observed the neatly tied back curtains, the perfectly placed sleeping bags and pillows, suitcases closed and lined up beneath the bunks, the dirt swept in front of the cabins. Jack Frankel came up and asked what I was looking for during inspection. I said, "Come along I'll show you." So we walked into the first boys' cabin. I had to face away from Jack so he wouldn't see my jaw hit the floor, as I was trying to figure out how to ask if this cabin was clean. Comparatively speaking, it was, (but compared to what?). Underwear hung off the ends of the beds, most of the clothes were at least three quarters of the way into the suitcases, a sleeping bag was hanging off one third of a bed, there were a couple of candy wrappers on the floor, but the middle of the room had been swept. Jack asked me what I thought. My mind was blank.

My favorite memories were as a counselor and working on the Summer Ministry Teams. As counselors we outdid ourselves under the direction, or the free reign, of Darlene Rigney—Darlene, Darlene the Whiplash Queen. We reached our pinnacle with the theme of Trading Places. We wanted the teens to gain an understanding of other situations in the world. Some of the days dealt with prejudice and

Mountain Top Experience

racism. During one lunch, everyone had to feed each other. One day was homeless day. Poor Gary, tall and athletic, had to survive on one bowl of soup. All the cabins were locked and we slept out on the volley ball court. A few campers were really shaken up as attitude awareness occurred when the blond-haired and dark-haired people were not allowed to associate. I was surprised when all the campers were able to sneak into the A-Frame with their Bibles for a secret Christian meeting without getting caught.

Along with the fun moments of fellowship and learning about God, we also shared some extremely difficult times. One of the worst was sharing God's love amid disaster. After dealing with Jon's accidental death, a much-loved camper came up to me and said, "We have seen your love and care for us and among each other this last week." I have learned again and again in life that to show an honest reaction of love and compassion is to demonstrate Christ's love for us.

Other memories include a counselor sleepover in Darlene's cabin. Matt came by and poured popcorn in front of the door. As the cabin got hotter and hotter, I thought it smelled of stinky feet. I was surprised to find that popcorn blocking the air path under the door was the reason. I recall being shaken awake during an earthquake while sleeping in the top of the old two-story lodge and then being told I talk in my sleep—the things you learn in community living. One time I thought I was being very responsibly calm when I told a fellow counselor of a bat in her cabin. She took her time to get over there and investigate the situation, and then was upset with me for not alarming her. I will never forget the many memories of being on the summer ministry team.

Ellen Koehler

Teen Camp

I remember going to the dining hall for lunch on my first day of Teen Camp, and there was a letter from home for me. Obviously, my thoughtful mom had mailed it even before I left, anticipating that I would need a hug from home. Joy and pride filled my heart, as I was the only camper to receive mail that first day. I received mail every day that week, too. Mom knew me well.

We used to go to the bowl for faggot services. That name has since been retired, and we are all glad for it, but the services still go on. A faggot is a bundle of small sticks. We would each take a stick, toss it in the fire and say a few words. These times were full of deep spiritual revelation, tears, and growth for most of us. I'll never forget them.

Liz (Dobbs) Favela

I don't want to give you the impression that the only things I remember about going to camp are the pranks and practical jokes, because I know of many campers who were influenced spiritually during those weeks. But, I recall an incident that happened one year at Teen Camp that maybe others will corroborate.

We were awakened one night by the sound of the bell ringing like crazy and Dave Crimi driving a tractor up to the boys cabins, kicking up all kinds of dust, shouting something about a fire drill, and ordering everyone to gather around the pool. There were lots of other activities going on that added to the anxiety of thinking there was a forest fire nearby, and we all hurried in an orderly fashion down to the swimming pool. Once all of the campers were assembled, some of the staffers (Dwight and/or Ralph Shirley et al), who had a fire hose hooked up to the hydrant by the retaining wall, proceeded to hydrate those not fortunate enough to realize we had been duped! I quickly understood

Mountain Top Experience

what the guys were up to, and lay down by the retaining wall near the hydrant to avoid being doused. Fortunately, the sprayers knew there was too much water pressure to point the nozzle toward me at such close range, and I stepped over the wall to get completely out of harm's way. Pretty rude of them, don't you think?!

Kevin Castleman

At what I recall was the very first Teen Camp (not at the same time as Family Camp) I remember exactly where I was sitting and what I was wearing in the group of about thirty teens gathered around the fireplace in the dining hall. I remember how I felt, who the speaker was, and the song we were singing when I responded to the invitation to publicly accept Jesus as my Lord and Savior. I remember afterward talking and crying and eating M&Ms with my friends in front of the snack bar. Thank you, Les Mark, for offering the invitation and Camp Maranatha for providing the place for a life-changing event I will never forget. I remember the last night of Teen Camp, throwing my stick in the fire, mumbling some promise and shedding lots of tears.

Nancy (Crimi) Beggs

I remember facing our mortality at the Teen Camp when the word was swirling around that Ginny Woodgate was very sick. I recall a summer of drought when God provided well water so camps could go on. In those teen years, I was, unknowingly at the time, discipled by the Shirleys, the Crimis, and the Glovers, and those in the Pasadena church who saw to it that everyone who wanted to go, got to every camp and retreat. I remember sleeping through my only earthquake in one of those tents at the upper end. Even today when I sing certain choruses, I am back in the Tabernacle or at the fireside at camp. I remember when I got

Teen Camp

caught sneaking out, that my dad (Joe Tom Tate), who was camp director, treated me just like he treated everyone else, even though I know he wanted to be much more severe.

I still have the scar from the huge splinter I got on one of the dining hall benches and recall the adventure of having the doctor in Idyllwild remove it. I remember as a camp counselor God using me to make a difference in a young person's life.

I remember it so clearly because, amazingly, the words that came out of my mouth were not mine. How I praise God for all those life experiences at Camp Maranatha that gave such good memories of teen years and such wonderful preparation for adulthood.

Roxanna (Tate) Sieber

With much thanks to my grandmother, Lillian Koehler, I never missed a camp or retreat all the way through high school. And I even have a file drawer full of pictures still unsorted. One day at Teen Camp, I got a lot of kids to pile up and make a rather large pyramid. Then I discovered I had run out of film. I feel lucky I made it out alive after that. The unflattering candids seem to have been my forte, so it is probably a good thing they are still unsorted.

In 1980, I was asked to be a Junior Counselor for seventh grade. When I arrived, the person that was supposed to be Senior Counselor could not make it. I found myself as a rookie in a cabin with nine seventh graders. I walked in the door only to get hit in the face with a pillow; a pillow fight was in full swing! Quickly grabbing two pillows, disarming two campers at the same time, I faced the other seven. The counselor actually won, and the week went great from then on. The kids were wonderful (believe it or not) and they even took most of the awards at the end of the week. I still have the trophy.

Mountain Top Experience

I kept at the camp counselor bit until 1986 when work was getting busy and it was harder to schedule time off. I was starting to feel old by then anyway. Until 1989, when I moved to Washington, I stayed active as a board member for the camp. I really enjoyed those activities, doing my best to make sure future kids could gain the experiences I had.

And yes, I stole the bell. Not once, but many times. In the mornings, it was not "Who took the bell?" but "Where did Sheldon put it?" It has hung from the rafters in the dining hall. It sat in the A-frame on a table. I tried to hang it from the rafters in the Tabernacle, but I could not find anything tall enough to get up that high. Good thing, I don't like heights. The best was when an unnamed fellow camper woke up one morning and asked why his bunk was wet. Only to see a cold bell, formerly covered with snow, sitting next to him.

I had help most of the time. That thing is heavy. The amazing thing was, I never got caught taking the bell off the roof. I always thought I was making too much noise. But I must have been quiet, as I ever so much wanted to join the counselors on watch in the dining hall and have a warm cup of coffee with them. I could see them while taking the screws out of the bell. Not even Big Bird (Bill Grey) heard me!

Dick (Beggs) did catch me the one night I decided to break into the kitchen and get a snack. I stayed cool the whole time like I was supposed to be there. He came in and got his own and told me to make sure it was locked up. Dick, I never did it again either! Speaking of food, I have to admit it was pretty good except for two occasions. One was when someone made pancakes out of baking powder by accident. They may have some industrial use, but I have no idea what. The other time was when these things that resembled rice were found in the mashed potatoes. I think the whole camp lost their appetite that night.

Those were the only two, so that leaves a great many good meals over 19+ years! Not to mention the good times we had. Fruit Loops still rule! 1 John 4:7–8

Sheldon Koehler

When I think about Camp Maranatha, it's impossible to pick just one special memory. My camp experiences mean so much to me I could write a small novel. However, I will try to keep to a more condensed version!

The greatest memory I have of camp is Teen Camp of 1987. That week transformed my life. The previous winter, my dad had died in an accident—December 22nd to be exact. He was unloading something from the back of his work truck when the emergency brake slipped. The truck was parked on an incline. We aren't sure if he impulsively tried to hold the truck back or if he simply did not have time to get out of the way, but he somehow got pinned between his truck and a huge oak tree. It was actually Dick Beggs who worked on reviving him in the ambulance all the way from Idyllwild to the nearest hospital in Hemet. But it was too late. He had been pinned too long and had suffocated. I have wondered if Dick might have prayed for my mom and me that day when we arrived at the hospital and were delivered the horrifying news. It was the prayers of those who cared that kept God's hand on my life, though I didn't know it at the time.

I was thirteen and, needless to say, full of questions, confusion, and very full of pain. My grief quickly turned my heart toxic and rebellious. I made some poor decisions and got myself in a lot of trouble. The only reason I even went to camp that summer was because my friend Katie

Mountain Top Experience

(Cruce Kelly) talked me into it. I arrived a very hurt and empty person.

That week at camp I remember we had to pair up with a "prayer partner." The very thought made me ill. My partner was Katie, but still I had no desire to pray, and I didn't even really know how to pray by myself, let alone in front of another person. Besides, I felt betrayed by God. That first day at camp was very long and awkward. I was within walking distance from home, so I was ready to just up and leave the next morning, but something kept me there. I know now it was the Holy Spirit holding me at camp. Through the tenderness of my dear friend Katie and prayers from other friends, I was able to let go of the intense pain I was harboring and give it to the Lord.

Later that same week, Katie and I were praying together so fervently we were saddened by the sound of the bell that signaled the next activity! I had never experienced anything like that before. There were a number of people that week who really experienced God's healing hand in their hurting lives. Words cannot fully describe the change in my heart and what I saw Him doing in the lives of friends around me was amazing. I felt God's love and the comfort I so desperately needed and I was drawn into a very real, personal relationship with Him, the One Who knows me better than anyone. He showed me that week, through His Word, He would be my Father and He would take care of me if I followed and trusted Him. Even though I didn't comprehend why I was now without an earthly dad, I just trusted that there was indeed a higher purpose I had yet to fully understand. The sorrow and sadness of my dad's death remained, of course, but deep destructive grief and bitterness were removed. Jesus truly took that yoke upon Himself and carried my burden. How real His Word became to me!

Teen Camp

I no longer saw His promises as being just for other people, but for me too. He has been so faithful to me.

What a blessing Camp Maranatha has been to me. My experiences at camp were the tools God used to unlock the heart of a hurting young girl and draw her into a relationship with Him. Every year I'm more amazed at God's greatness. My deepest thanks to all who served at camp. Truly the presence of God can be found in a humble little cabin on a mountain top not many have heard of. He can be found wherever and whenever a heart cries out to Him.

Carolyn (Schenk) Gillogly

One of my last years at camp I was on the Summer Ministry Team and I was at Teen Camp with the team. I was feeling a bit out of sorts. I knew I wanted to serve God, but felt that I had done some things that were more than God's forgiveness could cover. One night at campfire, I opened up to Darlene Rigney and told her what I was feeling. She was the team director and I was almost feeling like I shouldn't be on the team. She asked me what I had done to make me feel this way. I told her everything. Without judgment, she asked if I had asked God for forgiveness. I told her I had, but I wasn't sure if He heard me. I just didn't feel forgiven. She helped me make a list of everything bad I needed God to forgive me for. After I was done she told me to throw it in the fire. Then she said it's gone, it doesn't exist anymore in your eyes or God's and that was the last she said about it. Not once did she suggest I shouldn't be part of the ministry team. That was the first time I truly understood God's forgiveness and mercy.

Gwen (Koehler) Marron

Mountain Top Experience

You Can Teach an Old Dog "No Tricks"

One summer shortly before it was time to go to Teen Camp, a boy we'll call Bobby, announced to his parents that he was not going to camp. His parents were concerned by this unexpected announcement from their camp-loving son. After two or three days of concerned parental questioning, Bobby admitted it was because of a man we'll call Mr. Fun, one of the camp leaders. Bobby said Mr. Fun was disrespectful and abusive, always playing tricks on the teenagers. He described a trick where Mr. Fun would face one of the teenagers and while they were talking, someone else would get behind the teenager on his hands and knees. Then, Mr. Fun would surprise the first boy by shoving him backward over the person who was kneeling behind. Bobby said he had received an injury from one of those tricks last year and it had taken him six weeks to recover. He told his parents he had tried to talk to Mr. Fun about these tricks to no avail. Bobby and his friends had even tried pulling tricks on Mr. Fun, giving him a taste of his own medicine. But Mr. Fun just said, "Now boys, you shouldn't do that. You must respect your elders." Bobby had had enough of Mr. Fun.

The boy's parents knew their son was telling the truth. They knew Mr. Fun was a bit too fun-loving and perhaps a little rough with the boys. They had seen him do the very things Bobby had reported. This was a tricky situation. Bobby's parents knew they could talk to Mr. Fun about Bobby's concerns, but this might do more harm than good. They were quite sure that Mr. Fun would quit mistreating their son, but he would continue to play these rough games with the other boys, and he might even embarrass their son by mentioning in front of his friends that he was no longer allowed to play tricks on Bobby.

Teen Camp

Finally, they came up with a plan. Knowing that at camp Mr. Fun would often play touch football with the boys, they told Bobby that even though he was expected to respect his elders, that didn't mean he couldn't use all of his effort and skill when playing a game like football with adults. They carefully suggested that if Bobby were to find himself and some of his friends playing against Mr. Fun's football team, it would only be logical to do their best against the roughest player on the opposing team.

Bobby and his friends enthusiastically agreed to the plan and everything went as they had hoped. Well into a Teen Camp football game, Mr. Fun realized he was getting a beating. He called a time out and confronted the boys on Bobby's team about their rough play. The boys countered by bringing up his conduct and how he had mistreated them. Mr. Fun at last understood how they felt. He agreed to respect the boys in the same way he expected them to respect him (echoes of the golden rule?). That was the beginning of a great relationship between Mr. Fun and the boys (and a pretty good lesson on communication and creative parenting, too).

Walt Shirley

Service

The ministry of Camp Maranatha is not the result of any one man's work or gifts. It is built upon the efforts of many. With prayerful consideration, staff and committee members have volunteered and been selected. Couples, families and friends have made the trek up the mountain for a weekend of raking, painting, shoveling, pouring cement, sewing . . . In this way, we demonstrate the principles of 1 Corinthians 12:

> "There are different kinds of gifts, but the same Spirit. There are different kinds of service, but the same Lord. There are different kinds of working, but the same God works all of them in all men."

Perhaps, one of the greatest benefits of the hours of service given to Camp Maranatha, is the joy and companionship of the workers. Blistered hands, dirty fingernails, and the unique fatigue that comes after a day of sitting through board meetings bind us together in service to our God. Truly it is a privilege to participate in His work.

Serve wholeheartedly, as if you were serving the Lord, not men . . .
Ephesians 6:7

Mountain Top Experience

During the past two years, Camp Maranatha has been blessed by the volunteer organization MMAP (Mobile Missionary Assistance Program). During the fall and spring months, three to six retired couples arrive in their RV's (Recreational Vehicles) ready to work at whatever projects need to be accomplished. We have benefited in many ways from these skilled and willing workers. Their first project was helping with the completion of New Big Pine Lodge. Since then, they have contributed countless hours helping to build, remodel, repair, and refurbish many things around the camp. They have also been recruited for some much-needed office help. They are great people with a heart for service and love for the Lord. It is always a joy to interact and get to know each new group. We praise God for people like these who willingly give their time and energy to the ministry of Camp Maranatha.

Camp Maranatha Administrative Staff

A new command I give to you: Love one another.
(John 13:34a)

It's been pure joy working on staff this summer with people who live out what Jesus had commanded us . . . that is, to love one another! I have never been with young people who willingly work so hard together with such great attitudes. I know the Lord was your strength! And our wonderful adult staff and "bosses" added to the pleasure of working at Camp Maranatha.

I loved working with you all in the name of Jesus . . . and for His Kingdom!

Karrie Morlan
Staff Letter* - 1996

*Editor's note: See Lessons section to find out more about Staff Letters

Service

My husband, Otis, and I raked leaves at our first camp clean up. Charles was about two years old. The camp is roughly circular at the south end, and, on that weekend, he roamed freely around the grass area in front of Buildings 2, 3, and 4, the dining hall, and the horseshoe pit. He could run and play and keep an eye on us while we raked leaves, and we could see him.

I am grateful for the Sunday School Union that first introduced me to Camp Maranatha. I am grateful to Dorothy Luton who kept inviting me to the Bonita Avenue church and to that church for being active in camp cleanup. I do not think we have missed a work weekend since we first started participating. We have raked leaves, trimmed trees, washed windows, painted, removed grass and weeds from cracks in the cement at the swimming pool, cleaned the Tabernacle, stacked lumber, made and hung curtains, cleaned cabins, planted flowers, stacked benches on tables in the dining hall, worked in the kitchen, oiled buildings and benches, and sanded and finished chairs. I wouldn't trade a day of this for anything else.

Thank you Keith, Paula, and Walt Shirley for giving me the opportunity to work on the New Big Pine Lodge during its construction. Do you know how many buckets of water it took to get all that plaster off the floor? It was wonderful!

Jeannie Davis

Early in our marriage (1980s), our weekends were spent on camp projects that included tearing down the L-shaped building in the upper end, designing a new building for that spot, hanging trusses, and roofing what is now Building 6. I believe we may have even built another dam, or at least did some mending during those years.

Later, I remember our kids throwing up in their car seats coming to camp for work weekends. Now, we see them

Mountain Top Experience

helping around the camp as well. Timothy and Isaac helped take apart the old Big Pine Lodge and Ponderosa (only one tetanus shot required). Timothy helped roof the New Big Pine Lodge. Both boys now mow lawns and help in the kitchen and grounds.

One of our most recent memories is what we call "the last supper." All that remained of the Ponderosa was the chimney, so we set doors up on saw horses for a table, built a fire in the fireplace, and had a meal of hot dogs and s'mores before the chimney was pulled down the next day.

It is a blessing for our family not only to serve here, but also to be able to share parts of the camp together in this way.

Paula (Jaffarian) Shirley

My special thanks to all the workers who helped build the gazebo. I'm sure that Darlene (Rigney) would have been very proud to know that this special gazebo was built with love and in her honor.

Anna Mae Gardner

This past week I have been considering this summer and what lessons I will take out of it. One of the things that has been on my heart is servanthood. I have been trying to help some of you learn how to be better workers and thereby good servants. But mostly I have been focused on how I could be a better servant to you—not only to the other cooks or people over me, but to everyone.

Matthew 20:27–28 says, "... and whoever wants to be first must be your slave—just as the Son of Man did not come to be served, but to serve, and to give His life as a ransom for many." The best examples of servanthood we have at camp should be our bosses, the first among us. When I look at how hard Nancy works to keep the kitchen run-

Service

ning, I know that I am looking at a perfect example of a servant, and the same is true for Dick, Keith, and Paula. John 12:26 says, "... My Father will honor the one who serves me." Being a servant is more than something we do in the kitchen, and as we serve Christ in everything, we will be blessed.

This is getting long, but bear with me. Romans 12:10–11 shows us the way to be servants. Imagine how much God would be glorified if these were applied in the kitchen, or in the maintenance yard! "Be devoted to one another in brotherly love. Honor one another above yourselves. Never be lacking in zeal, but keep your spiritual fervor, serving the Lord." Galatians 5:13 adds, "... serve one another in love ..." Most of what I'm trying to say can be summed up in Ephesians 6:7, "... as if you were serving the Lord, not men."

I am glad to have worked with each one of you, and I thank you for your patience. I hope that I somehow managed, by the grace of God, to show you love in the kitchen, snack bar, or over meals. I pray that God will work in my heart further in being a servant to all of you. I have enjoyed every person this summer, maybe not completely, but I will go away with mostly good memories. Until next year ...

Sarah Paulson (Tate)
Staff Letter - 1999

The summer of '99 will live in my memory as a time of service, reflection, and fun. Camp Maranatha and I are old friends, and during my first days as Housekeeping Supervisor, or, as I prefer, "Toilet Queen," my eyes were lifted to the familiar peaks and ridges kissing the deep blue summer sky. I skipped to the upper-end bathrooms with a song in my heart and a mop in my hand, breathing deeply of the pine-scented air. Squirrels frolicked along leaf-strewn paths,

Mountain Top Experience

and birds soared among fluffy cotton clouds. My housekeeping staff was enthusiastic and eager to learn, happy to serve God by providing clean, tidy accommodations for the campers.

Then, like an earthquake, a cyclone, a flood, a democratic presidency, we were slammed to the ground by . . . General Clean-up! While no one has actually seen the General, he is known to be a harsh task master, frowning on harmless pursuits such as towel snapping wars in the front lawn or pink and blue cleaning solution fights. No, General Clean-up is never satisfied until the last weary staff member limps from the Tabernacle, Ice Cream Parlor, or bathroom clutching a dirty rag in a blistered hand.

Memories were triggered by seeing Tim, Isaac, and Larissa Shirley, of the days when I myself was a (pardon the expression) "camp brat." How I loved living in this beautiful place that others could only visit. Of course, I was always cheerful and happy to share my camp with the city dwellers who came for a brief stay. I sensed the campers were glad to see me, too, with the possible exception of the woman who came into the bathroom while my sister, Cary, and I were climbing over the stalls. This woman, who, by the way, did not live here, told us we weren't allowed to climb over the stalls. With the utmost charm and respect I quickly informed her, "We can do whatever we want. Our dad *owns* this camp."

Contrast this with Larissa, who volunteered to help me clean the bathrooms one day this summer. She did a great job, but I'm thinking she may need a few pointers on this whole "camp brat" thing.

Teaching the staff to sing "Rah, Rah, Potatoes and Ham" (*see Songs & Skits*) was a highlight of my summer. First sung in 1975, it brought to mind so many former staff kids who spent a summer or two at Camp Maranatha. How fun

Service

it was to hear this old standard sung to a bunch of hungry campers as they patiently waited for their food.

I was touched so many times during staff devotions. Along with the fun and laughter, we shared heartfelt prayers and spiritual insights. We walked with Bobbi and her family as they prepared for a kidney transplant. We shared the hope and sorrow of Nick, Seth, Carolyn, Robbie, and Michael as they fought against cancer. We cried with the camp director who ministered to a stricken counseling staff when one of his counselors had to be told her husband had died while she was at camp. We prayed for Shannon and Denny (Lazar), separated by so many miles, and for Jeannie (Oleson)'s mother who suffered a stroke. Hearing from camp directors and representatives reminded me that the work I did was more than scrubbing toilets or sweeping floors. It reminded me that I was serving men, women, and children who came here to see Jesus.

Yes, there were conflicts and momentary irritations. Perhaps my feelings were occasionally injured by the groans of despair that came from those assigned to housekeeping. But somewhere along the way, while toilets were plunged and floors were mopped, something greater happened this summer. Lives were touched and hearts were changed. I feel privileged to have played a part, however small, in the work God has done at Camp Maranatha.

**Jody (Beggs) Reeves
Staff Letter - 1999**

After retirement, in December 1993, we moved to Idyllwild. We wanted to be closer to some of our grandchildren (Larissa, Isaac and Timothy Shirley) and to the camp that has meant so much in the lives of many, including the life of our entire family. Again, we find ourselves offering assistance to the camp and campers in any way we

Mountain Top Experience

can serve. After thirty-two years on the Camp Maranatha Management Committee, Walt became chairman of the newly-formed Camp Construction Committee, which is a challenge he also enjoys. Much of his time has been employed in attaining a conditional use permit (CUP) for the camp which allows new construction. It took two years of constant work, jumping through many Riverside County "hoops." God answered many prayers for us, and it developed much patience and persistence for Walt.

Ruth Shirley

Special Guest
by
Jody Reeves
(written for Staff Devotions—see Lessons section)

"The sermon was really good today, don't you think?" asked Sara, exiting the sanctuary.

"Oh, yes," agreed Eliza. "Inspirational really, and so appropriate for today."

"Though I did notice," Rachel added, "*some* people weren't paying quite as much attention as they should."

All three pursed their lips and nodded solemnly. It was a pity, really, on such a big day, that the Miller boys had been chosen. *What was Pastor Tate thinking? It was well known those boys had no experience, and they weren't especially wise or spiritual either.*

"Having those two on the team just means more work for us," sighed Rachel.

"I guess we'd better get busy then," said Sara as the girls headed to the kitchen.

The lights were on, the ovens were preheating, and Sara was just filling the biggest pot with water when the rest of

Service

the team arrived. Vic bounded through the swinging doors, grabbed a towel, swung around, and snapped it at Sean Miller who jumped and smiled shyly. It was ten-year-old Sean's first year on the team, and he was glad to be a part of the group. Alex, Nicole and Tyler joined the others in donning crisp white aprons as Sara gave instructions. At seventeen, this was Sara's fifth year on the team and her first as team leader. She had been making lists for weeks, and had prepared a little speech to start things off right.

"First, I'd like to congratulate each one of you for being chosen. Your applications and recommendations showed you have the qualifications Pastor Tate looks for in his team members." She cast a doubtful look at the Miller brothers and continued. "As you know, the whole community looks forward to this dinner, and it is our opportunity, not only to raise funds for the orphans in Mexico, but also to be a good example of quality food preparation and service to the people who come for the meal. The kids who are chosen each year to prepare and serve this charity dinner have a big responsibility. We have a lot of work to do, and it is important that each one perform to the best of his abilities," she said looking in fourteen-year-old Vic's direction. "Check the list for your assignments and ask Rachel, Eliza or me if you need any help." She finished with a smile that she hoped looked both authoritative and friendly.

Eliza found her name on the list and pulled Sara aside. "Would it be alright if I made the salad? I've been studying new ways of cutting the vegetables. Anyone can do the rolls. The dough is frozen and pre-formed."

Sara listened thoughtfully. "Well, I guess someone else could do the rolls. I'll just have to change the list," she sighed.

Pastor Tate entered the kitchen. Everyone looked up to give him their full attention.

Mountain Top Experience

"I'm sorry to interrupt, but I want you to know we are expecting a very special guest today. It is more important than ever that everything go just right. You were carefully selected, and I am confident you will do a wonderful job." He smiled broadly, then left them to their work.

Sara broke through the group gathered around the list. "I just need to make one little change." She quickly erased Eliza's name after *rolls* and replaced it with Rachel's.

"Wait a minute," said Rachel. "I was supposed to make the salad. I don't want to do rolls."

"Don't be such a baby," Alex interrupted. "She's got me slicing ham. Rolls are easy."

"Oh, really? How 'bout a trade, then?"

"Sure, no problem and I'll be glad to trade dishwasher for pots and pans, too."

"No way, Alex," piped up eleven-year-old Tyler. "You were going to show me how to run the dishwasher. "I'm not working with a girl."

"Hang on a second," said Sara, frantically erasing and rewriting names. "One at a time. Vic, stop banging on those pots. It's not a drum set."

Vic slid the gravy ladle across the bottoms of the hanging pots one last time, then grinned at Sara as he put the ladle back on the shelf.

"Okay, I give up," Sara cried. "Everybody just sign up for something and get busy. You heard what the pastor said."

Before long, Eliza had Vic and Alex cutting heart-shaped carrots while she prepared the dressing. Sean and Nicole were setting up the serving area, and Rachel was telling Tyler how to make punch.

"I guess *I* can make the rolls," mumbled Sara. "At least everyone's working, now."

The kitchen was filled with sounds of chopping, slicing, and grating with only a few minor skirmishes until twenty minutes before serving time when Sara looked at

Service

the list. She felt a knot form in her stomach when she noticed there were some important items without check marks.

"Eliza, did you forget to mark the list after you sliced the ham?" she said, hopefully.

"No, I was still working on the salad."

Sara looked around the kitchen, trying to stay calm. "Has anyone seen Tyler?"

"Yeah, he and Vic went to the rec. room to play ping pong," answered Rachel. "I told them to make the cake, but they wouldn't listen to me."

"No one made the cake, either?" gasped Sara. She turned to Alex who was sitting on the counter trying to get a knot out of his apron strings. "Go get those boys out of the rec. room while I try to think of a dessert we can make in ten minutes."

"Okay, as soon as I . . ."

"Just go," said Sara in a voice that left no room for argument.

Eliza looked up from her salad bowl. Three hours of chopping, slicing, and carving had produced a beautiful mixture of lettuce leaves, radish roses, carrot hearts, and jicama curls. "I think there are some cans of pudding in the pantry we could use for dessert," she suggested.

Sara dropped her head into her hands, wishing she was anywhere else. The door to the serving area opened and Sean walked in carrying a rag dripping with red punch.

"Does anyone else smell smoke?" he asked.

"The rolls!" Sara shrieked and ran to the oven.

Fifteen minutes later, a line had formed behind the serving counter. Sean and Nicole smiled and assured everyone that dinner would be ready in just a few seconds. Rachel, peaking out from the kitchen, hissed to Sara and Eliza, "There's an old guy in a suit out there and he doesn't look too happy."

Mountain Top Experience

"That must be the guy Pastor Tate told us about," said Eliza, slapping together the last of the peanut butter and jelly sandwiches. It wasn't a great substitute for ham and rolls, but it was the best they could do. Sara grabbed the sandwich tray and headed for the serving area, followed by Vic carrying the cheesy potatoes, and Eliza with pudding cups. Everything was out on the counter when Nicole remembered the salad. Wrapping her arms carefully around the large bowl, she was about to back through the door when it swung into her.

"We forgot the salad," Sean shouted as a radish rose flew past his ear.

After that, the whole team seemed to be yelling or crying while the gray-haired man looked on in disgust. Sean dove under a nearby table and found his hiding place to be occupied by a boy of about eight. The boy looked frightened and confused.

"Wait here," Sean said and sneaked back to the serving counter where he grabbed a couple of sandwiches and some pudding cups.

The boy smiled when Sean returned with the food.

"Gracias," he said quietly.

The boys were soon giggling as they shared an under-the-table picnic and watched the chaos all around them.

With the last dish dried, the weary and discouraged team members were ready to go home. Pastor Tate again entered the kitchen. Every head dropped. No one wanted to see his disappointment. It had been his idea to let the kids prepare this meal. After tonight, the tradition would surely end.

"I just came in to congratulate you," he began. "Our special guest had a wonderful time and is anxious to go back to the orphanage and tell all the children about their kind friends in America. I wasn't able to be here for the dinner, but it sounds like you did an incredible job."

Service

The pastor looked out on a room full of puzzled faces. All except Sean Miller. He alone wore a surprised and delighted smile as he realized who had been tonight's special guest.

"Gracias," said Sean quietly.

"The king will reply, 'I tell you the truth, whatever you did for one of the least of these brothers of mine, you did for me.'" (Matthew 25:40)

My family and I worked together for only one weekend last year, but the memories of that weekend continue to bring smiles to our faces and warmth to our hearts. I'm so thankful the Lord has blessed me, my family, and everyone who has been to camp with the opportunity to share the love of Jesus in such a wonderful environment. I look forward to seeing familiar faces every year.

Melissa Matthews

After my husband, Tom, and I became involved with ministries apart from the Advent Christian denomination, Dave Crimi always kept us posted on activities at Camp Maranatha. We were excited to be a part of the decorating when the Ice Cream Parlor was dedicated and later the Darlene Rigney Memorial Gazebo. I am touched to be able to visit the gazebo when I am at camp and see plaques bearing the names of my sister, Sue Beardsley, my husband, Tom, and my aunt, Lillian Koehler. Their contributions to camp and the way their lives were touched by God at camp are precious memories for me.

Sara (Summers) Cruce

Camp Maranatha caught my attention in the early to mid 1960s when one day at a commission meeting I heard

Mountain Top Experience

one of the conference officers make a remark that shook me up. "We could sell Camp Maranatha, invest the money, and send every one of our Sunday school kids to any camp they choose to attend, using only the interest from the investment."

Until then, I had taken the camp for granted. I had been content with attending Family Camp, promoting attendance of the other camps by our Sunday school kids, and providing them transportation to and from camp. It was well known that the camp was having financial problems. Even though I wasn't sure that the officer was serious about this suggestion, it shook me up. The camp was not just a place to send our kids for a week each summer. Ruth (my wife) and I were raising three boys with the hope and intention that, when they were old enough, they would want to work on the camp staff during their summer vacations. We felt sure there could be no better environment for their first experiences away from home than working at camp under the supervision and protection of Errol and Juanita Hunt. Without Camp Maranatha that would not be possible.

So, not wanting to see the day when Camp Maranatha would have to be sold, we started looking for ways to get more involved. At that time, the A-Frame had been under construction for too long and progress was stalled after several volunteers had exhausted the time they had available. We started pushing for completion of the A-Frame and, as so often happens to people who get "involved," it wasn't long before I found myself on a committee. I was appointed to the Camp Management Committee and accepted the position of chairman a year or two later.

Walt Shirley

The Mountain Top! Undoubtedly my most favorite place on the face of the earth. A place for me, full of warm and

Service

pleasant memories, memories I can dwell on anytime I want. The memories come and go, often leaving me in tears. In my daily life, so many things happen to me that remind me of my experiences on "The Mountain Top!"

When I hear a certain song, when I hear a teaching on the famous love chapter (1 Corinthians 13), when I hear a teaching about David, I am brought back to a place where I love to find myself. Why? Because it is my favorite place on the earth. Undoubtedly!

When I was a camper at Camp Maranatha, working on the staff team was just a dream for me, and appeared very glamorous and attractive. In 1984, that dream came true. But it was far from being attractive and glamorous. All the kitchen work. The dishes. The bathrooms! All the work outside, the painting, and so on and so on day in and day out. Is it any wonder that the *other* staff guys sometimes played sick? OK, maybe I played sick once! OK, maybe even a couple of times. Or a few times? Hey, we were young and it was hard work! And Dick refused to pay us for those days anyway. It wasn't like we were playing sick and getting paid for it. But Nancy was always so nice and understanding, even though she probably knew what was going on. Anyhow, I ended up having so much fun I just had to come back for more in the summers of '85 and '86.

Of course, it wasn't the work that brought me back. It was a lot more. Dick and Nancy weren't just interested in having a few guys and girls up there during the summer to keep the camp running. I am convinced they were just as interested in our lives. They were interested in our growth, spiritually and emotionally, and I think that is why I always came back. All the Bible studies we had. Morning devotions every working day. These were some special moments. Oh, was I ever nervous on the days I had to do the devotions. But it was good for me. And I am very thankful for

Mountain Top Experience

those times. I remember Dick teaching about being a man after God's own heart like David. I'd never heard that before, and it continues to have quite an influence on my life.

There is one teaching that I believe ran through the veins of Camp Maranatha, and, I am sure, were I to work on staff next summer, I'd see the teaching is still running through those veins! The teaching about Love. You see, Dick and Nancy weren't just interested in having workers. Otherwise they would have complained and mumbled with us. Or they would have just managed the camp without the personal contact with us. No, they expected us to have a good attitude about whatever we were doing. They expected us to be patient and kind, not jealous, not boastful, not proud, rude, or selfish, not easily angered, and to keep no records of wrongs. They expected us to always trust, always hope, and to always endure. And this was, and I believe will always be, the central theme of Camp Maranatha. *Love, Love, Love!* For the Apostle Paul says without love we are as a blaring trumpet and a clanging cymbal. He says without love we are nothing. He also says we can give away all we have, but without love we have gained nothing. I needed to hear this back then. I needed to hear this, because there were days when all I did was complain and grumble about everything. Then, after hearing Nancy's paraphrases of 1 Corinthians 13, I had to admit that I'd accomplished nothing in my complaining and grumbling. But thank God for new beginnings.

Robert Underwood

Service

I CORINTHIANS 13—
CAMP MARANATHA SUMMER STAFF STYLE

If we could creosote all the railings around the camp in an hour, but didn't care about each other, our speed would mean nothing.
If we could cut croutons, make granola, and slice tomatoes with a wave of our hand and weren't polite and kind to the little kids, our magic would be worthless.
And if we could dig ditches, sweep the volleyball court, and split fire wood without getting tired, but didn't have a loving, serving attitude, our strength and endurance would be of no value at all.
Love is patient when the campers are late for their first meal because the bus broke down.
Love is kind when a camper needs special food because of allergies.
Love is grateful when we are invited to various homes for a progressive dinner.
Love is not irritable when we have to work extra hard before the health inspector comes.
Love is not jealous when the boys get to make dump runs and the girls have to clean bathrooms.
Love is appreciative when we get a weekend off to go to the beach.
Love is compassionate when a cut finger means a trip to the local paramedics.
Love is understanding when college student staff members need to leave before summer is over.
Carrot sticks, fruit trays, and punch on the tables will come to an end, but love is eternal.
General clean-up, working in the snack bar, and covering the pool will come to an end, but love never will.

Mountain Top Experience

Daily devotions, weekly staff meetings, and raiding the walk-in will come to an end, but love is forever.

Every year summer comes to an end, but love is everlasting.

Before we came to work at Camp Maranatha we weren't sure what to expect. But we have learned that a servant's heart and a thankful attitude are values we can take with us the rest of our lives.

These three things we will continue to learn: service, patience and love.

But the greatest of these is love.

Nancy Beggs

Guest Groups

Camp Maranatha has grown from a mountain retreat used only ten days out of the year for the Advent Christian "camp meeting" to a year-round facility serving 4,200 people from more than 100 different churches. Styles, programs, and formats may vary, but for every group Camp Maranatha is "A Place of Peace Where God Changes Lives."

Here is a glimpse into the hearts of some, outside of the conference, who have experienced the love and power of Jesus Christ here at Camp Maranatha.

Mountain Top Experience

I am a typical girl. Most of the stereotypes apply to me, and, hey, I'm not ashamed to admit it, either. So, one mention of the word *camp* makes my skin crawl. How my church got me to come here in the first place is beyond me. But when I did first come here in 1995, I was pleasantly surprised. I mean, there were beds, electricity, running water, and, best of all, clean toilets! There were still bugs, but when you're nestled up on a mountain you can't really do too much about that.

I had heard many horror stories from my mom about camp food. After I got through the accommodations, my biggest fear, next to being carried off by a swarm of mosquitoes, was starving to death. Once again, I reluctantly stepped out of my suburban comfort zone and sampled camp cuisine. It wasn't too bad. No, really, it wasn't. It was no Emeril Lagasse, but it was pretty good. I was just thankful I didn't have to starve.

For the first few days, I just thought that Denise Tamminga and Norberto Wolf had randomly picked a nice looking site to be dubbed "Camp Dunamis." It wasn't until later that week that I discovered we were actually borrowing a whole other camp site called Camp Maranatha. "Nice," I thought. But then, on my way back from a swim, I saw a plaque on a tree saying that this camp can only be used for God's purposes. And then, during cabin activities, I saw a plaque with a proverb* on it in front of the gazebo. I've always thought that was way cool.

So I'm still pretty girlie, but I will always remember the times I had here as a camper. Now, believe it or not, I am a counselor and can watch other junior highers grow up and experience God the same way I did at Camp Dunamis (a.k.a. Camp Maranatha). Dunamis is definitely using Maranatha for God's purposes.

Abby Craig

*Editors note: See "In Honor" section for the proverb.

Guest Groups

Camp Dunamis, directed by Denise Tamminga and Norberto Wolf, has been using the facilities of Camp Maranatha since 1989. Prior to that, they attended a very rustic camp with tent-like lodging and meals prepared by the group. "But a great spirit for the first multi-ethnic CRC (Christian Reformed Church) camp," says Norberto. They had about forty campers and four people on staff at their former campsite, and have grown to their present size of 260 (including forty-to-fifty staff and their families).

When asked to describe the focus of their camp program and how the camping experience has had a positive impact, Norberto told us, "Camp Dunamis has two foci: to bring middle-school youth to a personal relationship with the Lord, and to promote acceptance and love across cultural and ethnic lines. We want to prepare the way for the full family of God.

"Over thirteen years, countless youth from our group have seen their lives changed. Some counselors have been called to full-time ministry. Our present staff is mostly made up of former campers. Through all these wonderful experiences we have enjoyed the beauty of Camp Maranatha and the love of the staff!"

Jody (Beggs) Reeves

Camp Maranatha has always held a special place in my heart; not only because my brother and wife are directors, but also because their children grew up there. The second time I was there was for the 60th wedding anniversary celebration for my parents, Brad and Ina Beggs (that was in 1988). Many relatives near and far attended, and it was a joyful and wonderful occasion, if only for that fact. The planning and song writing and skit preparations were outstanding (but we've come to expect that from this bunch). The food and special decorations were the best, and Mom

Mountain Top Experience

& Dad were made to feel like royalty (rightly so). Dick, Nancy, Jody, Cary, and Kevin really outdid themselves as they planned and prepared and made schedules, etc. for two years prior to the big celebration. I will never forget the excellent accommodations, the fun times spent climbing mountains, playing games in front of a roaring fire in June, playing endless games of ping pong, giggling and sharing and enjoying each other, and letting Mom and Dad enjoy their time as they saw fit while they watched in wonder the fruits of their long and loving marriage gambol and play all around the camp, the swimming pool, basketball court, and various activities. The videos I took are permanent reminders of that very special celebration. Dad is gone now, and Mom, at 95, lives in a comfortable and well-managed nursing facility at Dowling Park. Dementia has taken away her ability to share good memories and to enjoy good conversations, but I am forever thankful to God for my parents and that He chose them to produce four pretty good offspring—and a whole crop of fantastic and wonderful grandchildren and great-grandchildren. Those wonderful days at Camp Maranatha will be forever burned into my memory and enjoyed over and over again. We thank God for Camp Maranatha and the ministry that has touched so many people for the Lord. And we thank Him for Dick & Nancy who are the very lifeblood of this very special place that God chose to tuck in the hills of Idyllwild.

Jean (Beggs) Snyder

Camp Maranatha is a camp that I look forward to going to every year. The camp grounds are always kept up, and the staff is always nice. In the fifteen-year period that I have been coming to this camp, I have loved being a part of the history. (My father, Larry Scott, used to come up and handle security for the youth camp.) At camp, children learn about

Guest Groups

God and about seeking God's will for their lives. I have grown spiritually here, and I love seeing the lives of children and adults change because of the presence of God in this place. As a child, I loved coming up to camp. I loved meeting other Christian children. As a counselor and staff member, I have enjoyed getting to know the camp staff, the counselors, the children, and Christ better.

One of my favorite memories is from Kids Kamp* 2000. My niece (Brittany Scott) was able to come up to camp for the first time, and I got to be there. Part of our camp program was to divide into teams and earn points throughout the week. That year, my team really understood the fact that as long as we hide God's Word in our hearts, we have the greatest treasure there is (winning was just a bonus!).

Kids Kamp 2000 is one of my best memories, because I learned that God would use me, even with all my imperfections. God knew that all this was going to happen before I was even born. All I have to remember is that God uses ordinary people like me to make something small into something huge.

God uses places like Camp Maranatha to aid in His plan and will. I thank God for all that this camp has done in my life and in the lives of all the campers that have attended here. I will always remember the way my niece would come running up and nearly knock me over as she jumped on me just to give me a hug. I will always remember the smiles on the children's faces when they received Christ into their hearts and learned something new that they had never heard before. I will always be grateful to this camp and for how God has used, and continues to use it, to minister to me and to countless other children and adults.

Lori Scott
Temple Baptist Church

*Not associated with the Advent Christian Southern Conference Kids Kamp

Mountain Top Experience

For more than a decade, four evangelical churches in Idyllwild have enjoyed a wonderful spirit of cooperation and interaction. We allow our shared love for Christ and our deep desire to see Him made known in our community to help get us past minor differences in style or doctrine. Three to four times a year these four churches plan activities that encourage shared ministry and fellowship together. Camp Maranatha has proven to be a great help in this regard. One event in particular has become an annual event, much anticipated by everyone, an event we simply call The Baptism and Deep Pit BBQ. From its inception eight years ago, Camp Maranatha has hosted this great afternoon of spiritual blessing, food, and fellowship.

Our churches begin to gather around 2:00 P.M. on a Sunday afternoon, and the children (and some adults) enjoy the pool while others play games and just chat. Then, about 3:30 P.M. everyone gathers around the pool (by now a crowd of some 200). We sing together, one of the pastors brings a devotional thought, and then each of the churches baptizes its candidates with all the other churches as witnesses to this wonderful act of obedience and commitment. When the baptism concludes, everyone moves over to the dining hall. Waiting there are tables covered with foods that each church family has brought, along with the main course of meat that has been prepared. With full plates of food, folks make their way out onto the grassy commons area in the center of the camp where they continue to mingle and fellowship. It all comes to a close about 6:00 P.M. Everyone leaves well fed and blessed to have been there. It is a highpoint of the church calendar for all of us. As the pastor of one of these churches, I am grateful for the generosity of Camp Maranatha as they share their facility with us. The camp and staff have enabled us to enjoy "the unity of the Spirit in the bond of peace . . . ," and we are thankful.

For the churches, Pastor Tim Westcott

Guest Groups

Chris Theile, a man in our church, was to be baptized at the community baptism service at Camp Maranatha. Pastor Bruce (Morlan) was explaining to him the procedures as his little son, John, stood nearby, listening intently. Later that day, little John, in an attempt to understand more clearly what his father was going to be doing, asked, "Daddy, when are you going to be marinated?" We all got a huge chuckle out of his question, and realized that at Camp Maranatha, baptism and marinated all kind of relate to each other!

Karrie Morlan

As a young person growing up in the Loyal Temperance Legion* and Youth Temperance Camps, I have visited Camp Maranatha for almost thirty consecutive summers. I have seen it grow and develop and have many fond memories of this beloved place.

I have watched the camp evolve with buildings going up and being improved, such as the A-Frame, the North Lodge, and the Snack Shop (AKA The Ice Cream Parlor). I have also observed memorable buildings disappear, such as the Big Pine Lodge, the Ponderosa, and the large open cabins in the upper end of the camp. Having been all over the camp, I have fond memories of the experiences and the encounters with God in these buildings.

I have seen Camp Maranatha develop into a place with many activities. From the surrounding hiking trails, with their passages to places such as the Idyllwild Visitors Center and the ominous "crashed car" (or Dead Man's Car), there is much to discover on the hiking trails. The softball field holds memories of many games and activities during the day. And, at night, looking up, it is a window to a beautiful night display of the heavens. The view from this place and the camp as a whole places one much closer to the

Mountain Top Experience

Lord where you can see yet another side of His beauty, majesty, and grandeur.

One cannot describe Camp Maranatha without mentioning the Beggs as caretakers. Their love for this place has always translated into a beautiful camping experience for so many people.

Camp Maranatha and Idyllwild will always have a fond place in my heart.

William L. Wilson

*The Loyal Temperance Legion is the children's division of the WCTU. The Woman's Christian Temperance Union (WCTU) was organized in 1874 by women who were concerned about the problems alcohol was causing their families and society. The members chose total abstinence from all alcohol as their lifestyle and protection of the home as their watchword. The organization exists in every state of the USA and in over thirty countries.

The Southern California WCTU has carried on the message to families through seminars in churches, scientific research and pamphlets, audio-visual material, poster and craft contests, and summer camp activities for youth, among many other programs.

The Southern California WCTU has sponsored the summer camp in Idyllwild at Camp Maranatha for almost fifty years. At camp, children and youth learn Christian values, healthy living practices, and abstinence from drugs and liquor.

For more information about the Southern California Woman's Christian Temperance Union, please write Colleen M. Wilson, State President, WCTU, 551 South Kingseley Drive, Los Angeles, California.

William L. Wilson

Guest Groups

King's Kamp first came to Camp Maranatha in 1989. Before that time, they used a campground in Big Bear where they had to provide, transport, and cook their own meals. There was no staff housing, and the campers slept in platform tents that got very cold at night and leaked when it rained. Recreation was limited to a volleyball court, because the majority of the site was built on a hill with no swimming pool or much else to offer the campers. They ended up bussing campers into Big Bear for various activities. They have found Camp Maranatha to be much more suitable for their purposes.

The focus of King's Kamp has always been to present the joy and rewards of being a Christian to their campers. They want them to come away from camp knowing that God loves them and that it is a good thing to follow the One Who loves them. They try to make King's Kamp a memorable experience that incorporates the fun and serious aspects of learning to walk with the Lord.

When asked how Camp Maranatha helps them to achieve their goals, Laura Hay answered:

"The Camp Maranatha staff has been an outstanding resource in helping us meet our goals. We have been blessed beyond measure by the wonderful relationships we have made through the years with Dick, Nancy, Keith, Paula, and so many others that make our experience at Camp Maranatha a great one. The staff has always been Christlike in their efforts to accommodate, welcome, pray for us, and love us. This makes the job of directing and administrating King's Kamp a pleasure. It is with grateful hearts that we celebrate this special fiftieth anniversary with all of you."

Kids Kamp

*Great Chief, Great Chief, Keeper of
the Mountain
Hear, oh hear our prayer
Hear our prayer for kind heart
Hear our prayer for brave heart
Hear, oh hear our prayer
Haiya kaiya haiya kaiya
haiya kaiya haiya kai
ya!*

Mountain Top Experience

The Legend of Chief Thunderbird

Many moons ago, in the shadow of the peak called Tahquitz, there lived a people of great strength and courage. The written word has not recorded their name. We know them only as The Mountain People, and, with one exception, they have long ago disappeared from this earth. It is the tale of that one exception that I tell to you this day.

Little Sparrow was the smallest and weakest in a tribe full of strong young braves. His mother, Gentle Hart, was the most beautiful and the most fragile of the squaws of The Mountain People. She did not live many years after the birth of her one scrawny and unpromising son, only long enough to tell to him the secret of The-God-Who-Loves. The Mountain People had many great and fearsome gods. Little Sparrow grew in the knowledge of the sky god, the god of war, and the tree spirit. Only Gentle Hart ever spoke of The-God-Who-Loves, and only to Little Sparrow in the small voice that was like the whispering wind.

When the Great Trouble came, Gentle Hart's spirit had long ago left her, and very few of her people remembered the fragile and beautiful mother of Little Sparrow. They did not know of The-God-Who-Loves, and, if they had known, it is doubtful they would turn to such a God in the time of the Great Trouble. Even Little Sparrow had forgotten the stories Gentle Hart had told him when he was still too small to sit away from the children's fire ring.

Chief Cunning Wolf was full of the gray hairs of wisdom. He called the strongest and most courageous of all the braves to the Council Teepee to speak of what might be done about The Great Trouble.

This, of course, did not include Little Sparrow. He sat away from the Council Teepee and looked at the deep blue sky and tried to remember the words of his mother, Gentle

Kids Kamp

Hart. There was something she told him, something she said about help against Great Trouble.

"We have many times faced and defeated our enemies," said Climbing Bear in the Council Teepee. "This time is no different. The god of war will give us strength."

The other braves agreed. "Let us paint our faces and do the dance of war. Then we will defeat this enemy as we have all others," said Climbing Bear.

And so the strongest and most courageous of all the braves prepared in the way of their fathers. Their painted faces looked fierce in the firelight as the dust rose up from their dancing feet. Then, in the first light of the morning, they ran up through Pine Woods, beyond Green Meadow, and into Dark Canyon to attack their enemy—only this enemy was not like the others they had faced and defeated. Their arrows and spears were powerless against The Great Trouble, and brave after brave fell in the onslaught.

With the shifting of the mountain breeze, the enemy turned away for just a moment, and those few remaining braves staggered back to their people who waited confidently for shouts of victory. Little Sparrow saw his brothers, their brave war paint smeared across defeated faces, and he knew there would be no shout of victory. If only he could remember the secret told to him by Gentle Hart so long ago.

Again, Chief Cunning Wolf called a council meeting. With many of the strongest and most courageous braves lost to the enemy, the gray hairs, those wise braves of the tribe whose strength had been lessened by many years, were also called to join the remaining warriors in the Council Teepee. This, of course, did not include Little Sparrow.

"We did not understand the strength of this enemy," said Seeing Eagle. We must seek the wisdom and power of the tree spirit to give us victory."

Mountain Top Experience

The other braves agreed.

And so they sang the ancient songs and walked with careful steps through Pine Woods, beyond Green Meadow, and into Dark Canyon where the enemy crept steadily toward the home of The Mountain People. The braves came to the trees that separated them from the approaching enemy and carved into the strong bark the ancient symbols of the tree spirit. Still the enemy came, and many more braves fell. Seeing they must run or die and leave their people unprotected, the few remaining braves jumped into the flowing waters of the creek of the strawberries and rode her currents home.

The wet and weary braves were not many, and their enemy continued to grow stronger. In the Council Teepee of Chief Cunning Wolf every brave who had seen twelve winters or more, whether strong or weak, gathered around their chief.

This, at last, included Little Sparrow.

"Our enemy is strong," said Chief Cunning Wolf. "He swallows our spears and arrows, he melts the trees with the ancient symbols, and he takes our strongest and most courageous braves. The god of war cannot save us, the tree spirit cannot save us. We must journey as a people up the twisting trail and beseech the sky god to save us from this Great Trouble."

Little Sparrow listened to the speech of Chief Cunning Wolf, and suddenly remembered the words of Gentle Hart. He remembered the stories she had told him of The-God-Who-Loves:

The-God-Who-Loves sent rain to cover the whole earth with water.

The-God-Who-Loves opened a path in the sea that His people might cross to safety.

Kids Kamp

The-God-Who-Loves multiplied bread for the hungry, sent sickness away, calmed the stormy sea and sky, and came down to walk with men.

The-God-Who-Loves met and conquered the great enemy, Death, and made a path to Life that all men might follow.

Surely, The-God-Who-Loves was stronger than the sky god and even stronger than the Great Trouble. But Little Sparrow kept these things in his heart and did not speak of them to Chief Cunning Wolf and the other braves. He knew they would not listen. He knew he was the smallest and weakest of all the braves.

The Mountain People took down their teepees, wrapped their young ones in animal skins, and followed the twisting trail to ask the sky god for deliverance from the powerful enemy. But the enemy came behind and snatched away the little ones from the back and enveloped the squaws in tongues of flame. The braves struggled on, coughing and sputtering, and still Little Sparrow spoke not of the things in his heart. When at last the remnant of The Mountain People reached the end of the twisting trail and shouted to the sky god, Little Sparrow fell to his knees and buried his face in the crumbling granite of the mountaintop. In despair he whispered a prayer to The-God-Who-Loves, "Please, send the waters from heaven and quench these flames of the enemy." Little Sparrow whispered these words over and over. He did not open his eyes until he felt the first drops upon his trembling back. The sky opened, and The-God-Who-Loves quenched the fire that had come against The Mountain People.

When Little Sparrow rose from his knees, he saw that he alone remained of all his people. "Why did you not tell us, Little Sparrow?" they seemed to say. "Why did you not tell us of The-God-Who-Loves?" Their silent pleas beat against the heart of Little Sparrow like a drum.

Mountain Top Experience

"I could not speak to you of The-God-Who-Loves," shouted Little Sparrow to the charred bones of his people. I am small and weak, and you would not have believed me."

Still the silent cries went on, beating like a drum. Little Sparrow fell once more to his knees and his heart cried out to The-God-Who-Loves.

"I am small and weak and afraid," he prayed. "But if I had another chance, I would tell them. I would tell them all the stories told to me by my mother, Gentle Hart. I would tell them that The-God-Who-Loves has defeated every enemy." Then, knowing there could be no more chances, Little Sparrow cried bitter tears of regret.

Softly, in the whispering wind, came an answer to his cry. "It is not too late even now, my child. Always there are people whose hearts long to know of The-God-Who-Loves."

The words that were not words filled the heart and mind of Little Sparrow.

"Though the lives of your people have been cut short, your life will go on. You shall always live here on this mountain, listening for the drumming call of the people who would hear of The-God-Who-Loves. You shall no longer be Little Sparrow, small and weak and afraid to speak the truth that lives in your heart. From this day, you shall be a chief, the only survivor of a people of great strength and courage. You are no longer Little Sparrow. You are Chief Thunderbird, bearer of good news."

And it came to pass just as the whispering wind had spoken to Little Sparrow's heart. Today, if you come to the place that sits in the shadow of the peak called Tahquitz, the drumming of your heart will call out to Chief Thunderbird. He will tell you how, long ago he called on the name of the Lord, The-God-Who-Loves, and was saved.

Kids Kamp

Through Pine Woods, Green Meadow, and Dark Canyon, he will come, the bearer of good news.

For, "Everyone who calls on the name of the Lord will be saved." How then can they call on the one they have not believed in? And how can they believe in the one of whom they have not heard? And how can they hear without someone preaching to them? And how can they preach unless they are sent? As it is written, "How beautiful on the mountains are the feet of those who bring good news!"
From Romans 10:13–15, Joel 2:32, and Isaiah 52:7

I was a counselor for several Kids Kamps when my mom (Marj Pitts) was one of the directors and stayed in the old Two-Story house. I remember at one camp *everyone* had the stomach flu—it was twenty-four hours, so no one was sent home. The nurse, Mrs. Barnes (Minihaha), had her hands full. It seems the camp before us had been sick and the cabins weren't cleaned efficiently, and so it went.
Bonnie (Pitts) Froehlich

I remember my mother being a counselor (Chief Red Squirrel) one year. I heard Debbie Drew (Miller) crying in the big house because she did not want to take medicine or something. I thought whoever was making her cry was horrible and fearsome. I think it was that nurse I later came to dread. (She inspected our hands at the dining hall door and never thought my hands were clean enough.)

Back when I was a Kids Kamper, we didn't have a pool. We would go to the stables at the end of the road and ride horses, or go in a truck to a pool somewhere in Idyllwild. My mother said I came home in the same clothes I wore there, and everything she packed was untouched in my suitcase!

Mountain Top Experience

I remember crying at campfire because I was too shy to go forward and throw a faggot in the fire and testify. Nikomas (a Mrs. Perry, I think) comforted me and told me I did not have to go. Then, at Kids Kamp in 1969, I did go forward and testify about how God had changed me, that I wasn't afraid now.

For a couple of my years at Kids Kamp, Sherrill Shoemaker (Brauer) was my cabin mate. We were not very popular, but we got along fine. For several years there were a couple of huge tree stumps where the fountain is now and we had a lot of fun climbing on them and sliding down!

Cindy (Howard) Bailey

Kids Kamp Memories:

Hearing Indian Stories told by "Big Chief" and knowing him as my dad.

Surprisingly, receiving the Little Chief Award when I was nine.

Riding in the back of a large dump truck with about 100 other kids traveling to another campground to go swimming. (Before we had our pool at Maranatha.) No seat belts, either!

Being taught to swim in that freezing mountain water by Lois Lobb.

My brother, Mike, being chased by a strange dog, tripping, landing on a sharp wire and cutting his leg, (he thought the dog had bitten him) and going to the town doctor for stitches.

Being Chief Chickadee.

Playing "HA" in the mission cottage with all the Kids Kamp counselors.

Campfires in the Bowl and inspirational services that touched my heart forever.

Debbie (Drew) Miller

Kids Kamp

Erik and I were shocked and honored to be asked to direct Kids Kamp. I didn't know what to expect. We consulted with our good friends Jack and Marilyn DuFour who had done this for so many years. Until you actually take on this tremendous responsibility, you can never be fully prepared. It was a lot of work but I enjoyed it immensely. It got increasingly harder for me to do anything because my son Joshua became so sick and was always in the hospital. So, after two years, we had to pass the torch. We had some great memories at camp. I remember at one Kids Kamp having a nice long hot shower with nice clean clothes on. Then, while preparing for closing ceremonies, a nice group of counselors threw the entire fifty-gallon container of ice water from the dining hall on me. I didn't know whether to cry or laugh.

Denise Stiers

My earliest memories of Camp Maranatha are as a kid sleeping in a tent before the cabins were built. I attended Kids Kamp and then, when I was too old to be a camper and too young to counsel, I helped my mom (Chief Wawona) with crafts. We were both thrilled the year "Big Chief Rick Drew" asked me to serve as a counselor for the youngest group of girls. As I reflect on that event, I realize that because Rick trusted me, a very young teenager, to handle the responsible position of being a counselor, it is now easy for me in my job at Camp Maranatha to trust teenagers to handle the responsible position of serving on staff. Years later, when Rick married Dick and me, we served on the Kids Kamp staff as recreation directors. As newlyweds we were named Chief Honey and Chief Moon. Thank you Rick and Camp Maranatha for the trust and the opportunities.

Nancy (Crimi) Beggs

Mountain Top Experience

For several years it was my privilege to share Kids Kamp. The program graciously listed my name as Chief Golden Eagle with a headdress to cover my head, but my friends soon learned to call me Chief Bald Eagle. We have often been seated with you in this Tabernacle which replaced the Tent. My eyes always seek the heights through the high picture window. The pines, for me, have pointed their green fingers toward the skies as the darkness soon clothes the light with the black garment of the night.

Up here, we view stars as they are never seen, shining so brightly above our smog- enshrouded cities in the valley below. The air here more rarefied, but clear and evergreen-scented, must soon be left for a different clime.

Rick Drew
July, 1969

My earliest memory of camp is standing in the registration line for my first year at Kids Kamp in 1970. I even have a photo my grandfather, Bill Koehler, took of the event. Another kid and I are obviously having fun already! And I have no idea who he is.

Sheldon Koehler

Kids Kamp was the highlight of the year for us. It was a great place to be a kid.

Dini Walters (McGregor) and Cyndi Walters (Sapwell)

I have many warm memories of my time at Kids Kamp, as I'm sure everyone does. Exploring the mountains, singing in the Tabernacle, running down the gully dressed as Indians on the last day to see our parents again. Oh, and buying things at the snack bar (without having to get parental permission!). One night during my first year, I got to take part by playing the Indian drum down by the teepee.

Kids Kamp

I'll never forget the feeling of excitement and pride I experienced participating in that extraordinary ceremony!
Rob Hopper

Memories of Camp Maranatha remind me of my spiritual home. I recall my older brother (Sheldon) packing and going off to camp. I remember being scared of meeting new people the first time I went. However, I can say that I have always been accepted and treated with love. The name of Big Chief was intimidating to me as a third grader. At campfire for the first time, chanting for Chief Thunder Bird was spooky. Being rousted out of bed for a midnight hike was an adventure.

Future counselors need to know that the third graders are the least likely candidates for sneaking out of the cabins on the last night of camp. By the end of the week, if you have done your job right, we are just too exhausted.
Ellen Koehler

Being a camper at Camp Maranatha has always been a special experience for me. I could write about hundreds and hundreds of wonderful experiences as a camper, but I think the most wonderful and most important experience was my conversion in the fifth grade.

It was after the evening bowl service. I asked my counselor—"Chief White Cloud," I believe—if I could receive Christ into my heart tonight! All he said to me was "Okay, we can talk later when everyone is sleeping." He somehow misunderstood me and thought I just wanted to talk. Anyhow, later we went to the Tabernacle and there I gave my life to Jesus.

One may ask "And where is the great experience?" The great experience was that as of that moment when we finished praying, a "light" entered my life. A light that has

Mountain Top Experience

been with me ever since. It wasn't a bright light, but it was there. I even remember that the Tabernacle got a degree lighter. It is an experience I don't talk about a lot, but when people ask me when I was born again, I can say a warm August night, in 1978, on "A Mountain Top!"

Robert Underwood

Pastor Jim Smith (a.k.a. Chief Thunderbird) was our fearless leader at Kids Camp. At fireside in the bowl he would emerge from the darkness with a war whoop, charging into the bowl, dance around the camp fire, then sit and tell Bible stories with an Indian theme. I'm not sure, but I think Pastor Smith had a brother, Jack, who was usually the chief of the Mustang tribe.

I have a funny story to tell about a prank that I, and a friend (Jackie Carlton) played the last morning of our last Kids Kamp in August of 1967. I don't know if there is still a bell atop the office, but, at that time the staff would ring it in order to announce certain events in the daily routine. Of course, it was the object of much scorn when it was used to awaken campers to start their morning. Even at an early age, some of us resisted becoming Pavlov's campers! Jackie and I kept each other awake all night, and, before dawn, sneaked out of our cabin and used our counselor's beach towel to stuff inside the bell (around the clapper) to keep it from ringing that morning. That accomplished, we climbed in one of the back windows (which we made sure was unlocked the night before) of the Ponderosa, and waited for the staff to perform their morning ritual. We excitedly awaited movement of the bell to see if our mission was successful.

Our efforts were more than rewarded. The bell began to swing. Then it swung more violently as the staffer realized there was no sound resulting from the pull of the rope. We learned later that that staffer had at first thought the bell

Kids Kamp

had been stolen, but, after walking outside the office, realized that it was our stuffing that impeded the ringing.

Of course, the towel, which they recognized as belonging to our counselor, was booked into evidence, and a mock trial was held forthwith. Our counselor was acquitted when: 1) it was determined that he had no motive to allow the campers to sleep in, and 2) we testified that he was sound asleep when we took his towel that morning.

Jackie and I were pretty groggy the rest of that day.

Kevin Castleman

My stand-out memory of Kids Kamp is meeting my dear friend, Gene Crimi. I was six or seven and Gene was eleven or twelve. He was standing on the porch in front of the office surrounded by girls. I'm talking *girls*. There were at least fifty. Gene was wearing a white sweatshirt that was just like one I had at home. It said Aurora College on it. My first impulse was to impress this big kid with my impeccable genetic background. I confidently elbowed my way up to where he was standing, pointed to his chest and announced, "My uncle is *dean* of that college." Gene looked at me in a way that I would later learn only Gene can and said, "*My* uncle is the president." And he wasn't even lying. As he and his entourage glided away, I made up my mind that I would spend the rest of my life attempting to pattern myself after him.

Jamo Jackson

I was a reluctant camper at age nine, but after my first Kids Kamp, I was hooked. Through my childhood and teen years, as a camper and as a counselor, I went up to Camp Maranatha every chance I got. I remember: In a camp full of Indians, Everal Shelton and I wore cowboy hats the whole week (that's as rebellious as twelve-year-olds got back then).

Leslie (McIver) Hutchins

Mountain Top Experience

When my daughter Katie was old enough to attend her first Kids Kamp, it was with tears of joy that I looked forward to her being the beneficiary of the same spiritual blessing I had first experienced twenty-five years before. Weeks at camp in the summer and retreats during the school year became character-building landmarks for her, just as they had for me.

Sara (Summers) Cruce

I heard Barb (Smith) Taylor tell Debbie (Drew) Miller, eight-year-old camper, "I'll never make Little Chief. I have freckles and they never choose anyone with freckles!" (Both girls made Little Chief, freckles and all.)

Marie Drew

"Where's Nancy?" This question has been asked by hundreds of campers, friends, and family. Whatever problem one has before him, Nancy can find a way to fix it. This is how she has always been and always will be, a mother, grandmother, and best friend to all. For me she has played the role of grandmother . . .

"Good-bye, Mom." After I had repeatedly assured my concerned mother I would be fine, she finally, reluctantly, left me to spend an entire week away from home. The week of little Indians, pool time, and a daily dollar's worth of goodies flew by. You've never seen such a thrilled, independent third grader, that is, until Wednesday. I remember clearly, it was free time and my counselor was giving us all new hairstyles. When she had finished, one of my fellow cabin mates asked me, "Whose hair looks best, Katie?" Not knowing the rules of complimenting, I gave my loyal but honest opinion. "My best friend, Ashly's." Obviously this was the wrong answer because, let's call her Susie, ran to my counselor and told on me, for what, I'll never know.

Kids Kamp

But it must have been bad, because my counselor began to reprimand me—much too harshly for my seven-year-old spirit.

This tragic event not only shook me, but ignited an ache of homesickness for my mother. Reduced to tears, I was comforted by faithful Ashly. She hunted down my older sister who patted my back and quickly left to chase boys. Unsatisfied by Amy's effort, Ashly took my hand and dragged me away. Our destination was the camp office where her grandmother—and my savior—Nancy, sat waiting to solve all my problems.

Ashly announced me and my problem matter-of-factly. "Grandma, this is Katie and she misses her mom."

I can't remember exactly what was said in that warm log cabin, but that grandmotherly smile and hug vanquished all my sorrow. The fragrance of her skin during that hug stays with me still today. I'm sure this story is not a surprise to any who have met God's wonderful servant, and many of you may have a similar story. I believe I can speak for a large number in saying what an amazing gift God has given to us and to the camp we all love. Thank you, Nancy.

Katie DeRoche

I remember that Rick was Big Chief when our son, Paul, was a camper at Kids Kamp. Paul worked very hard each year to earn a Little Chief Award and finally got it on his last year at Kids Kamp! He and Gene Crimi have had a running argument for years, because Paul says *he* deserved it the year before. But Gene won the sympathy vote because he had gotten sick with the flu during the week of camp.

At Paul's graduation from Aurora College in 1970, he went over to Rick, unzipped his graduation robe and re-

Mountain Top Experience

vealed his Little Chief Award underneath. Rick got a big laugh out of that, but Paul assured him he always wore it for "special occasions."

Marilyn McIver
(As told to Marie Drew in a letter written shortly after her husband, Rick Drew's, death)

Poet's Corner

"Maranatha—Our Lord Come"
Sighs sweetly on the breeze
And hearts are filled with poetry
Like needles on the trees

Scoff not at these poetic ones
Read every word with care
And see if your heart also has
A poem written there

Mountain Top Experience

Dear Lord,
    I think I've learned the true meaning of "friendship" this summer.
    One of Your special children helped me learn what friends are really for,
And what a difference they make in our lives.
She has helped me conquer my fear of other people,
And has taught me how important it is to have someone to share my joys and sorrows with.
She loved me when there was no reason to love me.
She listened when I needed to talk,
And when I didn't,
she kept me talking and laughing
when I felt more like crying and giving up.
She shared her secrets
And held me close
when I needed it the most.
How can I ever show her all the love she's shown me?
Or tell her how much she has done for me?
It would take a miracle for me to do this, Lord.
But I pray that I will develop the love that You have shown me,
through people like this friend of mine,
And that someday I will be able to help someone else as much as she has helped me.

Karen Rigney
Staff Book - 1981

When I am lonely and sad
I go to the mountain
Where my comfort is found
When the world is too big
I go to the mountain

Poet's Corner

Where I can hear my heart pound.
When I have no more to give
My God will give me
The mountain of His love.

Denise Stiers

Wishing on a shooting star.
That You will send the words to describe this summer.

But how can I explain a time when pain means growth
And loss brings gain?

When happiness is brought by a bird,
Seeing old friends and making new ones.

A time when frustrations bring on growth
Because You have shown me how.

Learning to live with others
Sharing their pain and confusion
Wallowing in their happiness
Sharing their belief in You

Watching them grow,
Then realizing I've grown too.

The time seemed so long when it began,
But at its end has flown by.

Now the time has come to leave this place,
The place where I have grown so much,
The place where I have grown in God.

Mountain Top Experience

Time to go home,
But it will look different

Because I am looking through different eyes,
Eyes that have seen pain and joy,
And have accepted both with Your help

I'm not the same person anymore
I've changed for the better

I've learned the best,
and the hardest lesson anyone could learn,
That no matter what happens,
God will always be there to help me.

Your lesson this summer will make my life easier.
It was a hard lesson to learn
But it was worth it.

Susan Reimenschneider
Staff Letter - 1984

Read the story behind the poem in "Impact."

In the beginning, the first day,
All of us gathered here,
Each one from a different background
Called for the same reason
To be a servant for the summer.
Without knowing what everyone else was like,
We united to form a team,
And through our servantship
And reverence for the Lord
Our own special family soon formed.

As the days and weeks went by,
Members of our family were faced with reasons to cry—

Poet's Corner

There was the loss of a loved one,
And the question of "How could a father just leave?"
But our strength and love for one another
Was all that one of us could need.

Now as the end draws near,
We are faced with one more difficult situation.
Now we must let go and simply "Let God."
At first we couldn't imagine life with one another
Now we can't imagine it without everyone.

Just remember God and His words,
"I am with you, I will not fail you nor forsake you!"
Through Him and His love we will always be together,
For we know His promises are true.
Derri Knowles (Ironfield)
Staff Letter - 1988

The love of God surrounds us
Like the air we breathe around us
As near as a heartbeat as close as a prayer
And whenever we need Him, He'll always be there!
Cathie Coe (Davis)
Staff Letter - 1988

Friends and Foes

I see the faces, some are new.
Life is beautiful, up here with you.
Work is great, refreshing, fun—
We are a team, under God like one.

As weeks go by some things wear thin,
And sometimes we get under each others' skin.

Mountain Top Experience

But still we laugh and joke and kid,
And we confide what we thought and did.

We're the best of friends, and biggest foes,
And how we all lived here—He only knows.

We're a family for a summer, or maybe more,
If only some would leave open the door.
I look at the faces, before me here,
Familiar faces, that have become so dear.

The summer's fading and fading fast,
Oh how I wish somehow it'd last.

It's been great, and it's been bad,
And sometimes, too, it has been sad.

But most of all, it's been learning how
To serve the Lord and others now.

We're the best of friends and biggest foes—
And, each day now someone goes.

We'll soon depart to our separate homes
With summer becoming just a memory
And we'll remember the sweat, boredom, and tears,
But we'll also miss each other—you'll see.
For we *are friends*.

Candee Wright (Schreiner)
Staff Letter - 1986

Poet's Corner

A place so like heaven
yet earthly in its disguise.
It brings love to lonely
hearts
like warm firelight
brings to a dark rainy
night.
It gives fulfillment
to the empty,
pathways to the lost.
This place binds
hearts together with
strong ropes twined
with love, peace
and cheer.
In days alive only in
memories,
it gave joy that released
a child's weary mind
so toiled from pains
of growing.
Now this place lifts
me
high in its altitude
to touch the stars,
the clouds,
the rain,
and God's love
shown through
sunbeams that filter through
treetops and
people like *you*.

Jane Gransee (Mergens)
Staff Book - 1982

Mountain Top Experience

What this summer meant to me
Let me see
The boys staff was great
They were seldom late
Which is something to celebrate.

What did I think of the rest of the crew?
Besides the fact that most of them were new.
I thought they did their job very well.
But I was outside, so it's hard to tell.

I love spending time with my kids and my wife.
Most of it was fun and caused me no strife.
I've really enjoyed working here,
But must confess I'm glad the end is near
So I can relax and have a Coke.
P.S. That last line was only a joke

Joe Reeves
Staff Letter - 1988

    This one's for all of you, to show how much I care, my thank yous say so little, yet mean so very much.
    The times we've shared together, I will cherish in my heart. You're my shining star, I pray our lives will never part.
    The laughter and the smiles you've given to me so freely have brightened many days and your hugs of love and comfort have warmed me from inside.
    We've even shared some tears together, trying to ease the pain.
    Yet, from this comes a learning and growing experience, from which we both have gained.

Poet's Corner

I've found honesty and an understanding truth in you, something that is quite rare, yet by looking in your eyes I know it's because you really care.

You've brought about new emotions, stirring up old ones too, causing me to dig down deeper, finding out what's true.

You've taught me the difference between loving and hating. You've given so much of yourself to all of us, never asking for anything in return. You're the greatest who's given me fantastic memories of a great summer.

But thank you most of all for being what you stand for, and most importantly, who you are to me.

Patty Rabell-Moreau
Staff Letter - 1984

To Give You Glory

A song inspired by a message shared by Grant Jaffarian—see what he had to share in "Impact."

Verse one:
Precious Lord, what can I do?
There is nothing I can add to You.
My only prayer, my one desire,
Is to live that I might lift Your Name up higher.

Chorus:
To give You glory, to praise Your Name, to serve You only, Your love proclaim,
To show Your mercy, to do Your will,
Lord, shine through me, I'll be Your beacon on a hill.

Verse Two:
Holy Lord, how can it be
that You should care for one as small as me?
If You find joy, within my praise,
I will worship You for all my days.

Mountain Top Experience

Verse Three:
Let my light shine in such a way
that men might see my good works and they'd say,
"All glory to the Lord on high.
We will raise His praises to the sky."

Repeat Chorus

**Jody (Beggs) Reeves
Summer 1999**

Camp is a Home . . .

When the city gets too tough
and you have to get away
for a week, or even just a day.

Camp is a Home . . .
When you have a problem
and you don't know what to do
you go to camp to think it through.

Camp is a Home . . .
It's a godly place
and the staff is a chosen few.
I had the opportunity to serve and my
brother and sister did too.

Camp is a Home . . .
Where we spent the summer
serving people from near and far.
And at the same time
learned more about who we are.

Poet's Corner

Camp is a Home . . .
Where we were a part of the Beggs' family
As they set an example of how
Christians should be for all the staff
and visitors to see.

Camp is a Home . . .
Zann is a part of the family too.
She's the one who tells all the girls what to do,
to prepare the food for all to eat
including the camp that was in for the week.

Camp is a Home . . .
Where my Christian life came to start
and so much I wanted to give my part.
Camp Maranatha will always have a
special place in my heart!

Darlene Rigney
Staff Book - 1981

Camp Staff

We are one in the Spirit, we are one in the Lord
We are one in the Spirit, we are one in the Lord
And we pray that all unity will one day be restored

And they'll know we are Christians by our love, by our love
Yes, they'll know we are Christians by our love

We will walk with each other, we will walk hand in hand
We will walk with each other, we will walk hand in hand
And together we'll spread the news that God is in our land

And they'll know we are Christians by our love, by our love
Yes, they'll know we are Christians by our love

We will work with each other, we will work side by side
We will work with each other, we will work side by side
And we'll guard each man's dignity and save each man's pride

And they'll know we are Christians by our love, by our love
Yes, they'll know we are Christians by our love

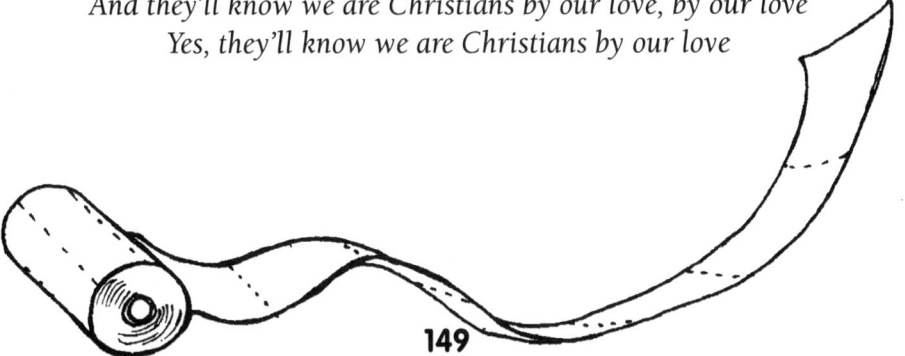

Mountain Top Experience

As I reflect on Camp Maranatha's history and the thirty-one years I have been a part of this ministry, I realize my love for Christian camping began long before God called me to this place.

My first experience as a camper was at Camp Suwannee in Dowling Park, Florida, in 1953. I was nearly fifteen years old. I had not been away from home much, and I remember that wonderful feeling of freedom and independence as I attended a camp for the first time. I may have been a bit too exuberant and had a little too much fun that first year, but still I remember camp as being this exciting place with a rope swing over the river, a ball field near the woods, girls' cabins to raid, and the Suwannee Bowl (campfire meeting). I learned more about God and encountered adults who really cared about me. Right from the beginning, I loved camp. A couple of years later, I was asked to serve as Camp Master and then, at age twenty-two, assistant director of Camp Suwannee Teen Camp.

As I look back, I recognize the impact that early camping experience had on my life. Friendships, spiritual growth, silly skits, swimming and hiking, those are all great memories, but camp provided for me a place to grow up. I arrived at Camp Suwannee a young, insecure, energetic teen. But two young men, the camp director, Travis Carter, and my first counselor, Pomeroy (Punk) Carter, saw in me potential that not many others saw at the time. Over those next few years, they gave me leadership positions, treated me like a responsible person, and helped me develop a sense of worth. More than anything, the feeling of being trusted helped me become a responsible person, and that is very important to me to this day. I came to Camp Suwannee as a kid, and after several summers was a part of the camp staff, helping insecure, silly teens begin to grow up. I'm sure I would have continued my involvement with Camp

Camp Staff

Suwannee, but after graduation from college, my stint in the Army Reserves, marriage to Nancy, and subsequent move to Illinois, it was impossible. However, the dream did not die, and I hoped that some day I would return to the work that I loved.

Meanwhile, we began our life in Aurora and my career in the business world. We immediately got involved with the local church and soon were directors of the Junior High youth group. We volunteered at Camp Rude and planned for an early retirement so I could return to the Christian camping ministry. But God's timing was a little different. Just ten short years later I was hired as the new manager of Camp Maranatha to follow Errol Hunt. On August 1, 1970, we (Nancy, Jody, Cary, and I) rolled into camp with a truck and a car and two U-Haul trailers that contained everything we owned. After settling in the old Taylor Cottage (Where the Shirley family now lives) I began work on September first. Fifteen months later, Kevin was born.

Living at Camp Maranatha and Idyllwild was a great place to raise a family. All three of our kids benefited from growing up at Camp Maranatha. They learned a variety of practical skills while working on the camp staff, and they learned people skills by living and interacting with camp guests. They enjoyed the many benefits of camp life and have wonderful memories of being camp kids. The greatest joy of all for me has been working with my wonderful wife, Nancy, in the service of the Lord.

I am still excited about Christian camping. I know of no better way to reach kids for the Lord or to teach them important basic living skills. We try to lead the same way the Carters did: believing in young people and giving them the opportunity to develop both work skills and spiritual skills in a loving, supportive Christian environment.

Mountain Top Experience

It is rewarding years later when these former staff "kids" return for a visit or to enroll their own children for a week of camp or to bring us a second or third generation summer staffer. The legacy of Christian Camping is far-reaching. Camp Maranatha has been a part of this vital ministry for fifty years. I have been blessed for over thirty years to share in this ministry, and I pray that God, in His wisdom, will continue to bless Camp Maranatha as we seek to provide "A Place of Peace, Where God Changes Lives."

Dick Beggs, Director

A TRIBUTE TO SUMMER STAFFERS

Every summer you arrive with enthusiasm and excitement, a willingness to serve, an abundance of energy, and a heart for the Lord. You come from as close as Idyllwild and as far away as Hawaii, Florida, Georgia, Vermont, and Illinois. You teach us patience, acceptance, and unconditional love. Together we learn about trust, faith, and endurance. We work and play, pray, laugh and cry. By the end of summer we have come to appreciate your individual gifts and skills, and it is hard to say good bye. You enrich our lives beyond measure.

We are additionally blessed by those of you who continue to stay in touch. Thank you for e-mails and notes, graduation announcements, wedding invitations, Christmas cards, and pictures of kids and even grandkids (ouch!). Thank you for taking time to stop in and visit. Thank you for coming back to help out in the kitchen and on other projects around the grounds. Thank you for your financial gifts and your prayers. Thank you for sending your children to attend summer camp and for encouraging them to serve on staff. Over and over our lives are blessed as we

Camp Staff

observe the continuing impact of the ministry of Camp Maranatha.

We are forever grateful to summer staffers past, present and future. May God bless each of you with camp memories that lift your spirits and bring you joy.

Nancy (Crimi) Beggs

In the summer of '75, the staff guys were at the upper end of the gully with the tractor. We were using it to transport and dump bricks to fill in some eroded spots in the gully. Keith (Shirley), being the senior summer staffer, drove the tractor. I was giving directions, moving him close enough to the rim to dump the bricks over the edge.

I had Keith perfectly positioned on the lip of the gully, when the weight of the bricks caused the bank to give way. Keith stood on the brakes, riding the sliding tractor all the way to the bottom.

We had to use the wench on G.I. Joe (the large military truck) to get the tractor back out. Needless to say, Dick wasn't too pleased. (Seemed he wasn't too pleased with a lot of stuff that summer.)

I think Dick took it out on us the next summer, as we were sentenced to hard labor, reclaiming used blocks during the rebuilding of the bowl.

Dean Hardi

The gentle whirring of the golf cart and wind blowing through my hair inspired me with a sense of freedom as I steered my way to the North End. A fistful of staff keys made me flush with feelings of responsibility and authority. And the stiffening smell of the Pine-O-Lav I was about to splash around the upper end bathrooms kept me grounded firmly in reality.

Mountain Top Experience

As I pulled up to the bath house and parked my sled (that green three-wheeler monster was one sweet ride), I was undaunted by the prospect of muddy floors, unflushed toilets, and dirty sinks that were holding onto hair as if it were dear life itself. It was a sunny, breezy Thursday morning, and I couldn't think of anywhere I'd rather be.

After making a trip to the storage room which, of course, was only accessible to those at the highest level of authority, I headed for the girls' bathroom. I gave two firm blows to the door and then, with all the manliness I could summon, bellowed, "Staff! Anybody in there? I'm here to clean your toilets!"

The work went quickly and soon I found myself starting in on the boys' side. Why was I so happy? This wasn't exactly the stuff of dreams, and yet I was more contented than I imagine any prince or player could be. As I began mopping the shower stalls while contemplating this mystery, in ran a little junior camper with a Bible in one hand and a lizard in the other. "Could you hold these for a minute? I've got to go pretty bad. Thanks, I'm late for Bible class."

As I stood holding the squirmy reptile in one hand and the Good Book in the other, it became clear to me why this caged bird was singing. I was in service, full service, to my King on His campground where He was doing His Kingdom work in the lives of so many. What a wonderful feeling of fulfilled purpose entered my soul! There was nowhere else I'd rather be.

I headed back to the kitchen with my heart full of joy, my nostrils enjoying the sweet smell of pine, and my head filled with thoughts of volleyball.

John Tate

Camp Staff

Usually my summer ends and I am half-ready to go home. This year is somehow different. I wanted to draw out my stay as long as possible and savor every minute of camp, from Saturday clean up to nights in the girls' staff house (or outside wreaking havoc!). Camp Maranatha is in my blood, I think, and I am eternally grateful that I was able to spend another summer there, especially because I waited until the last minute to decide about it! Thank you to everyone who always makes camp such an incredible bonding and growing time. Especially Keith, Paula, Nancy, and Dick. You all make camp what it is, and without you it wouldn't be nearly as exciting! I'm here in New York thinking about how I miss this summer, and I can't wait to visit next year. God bless all of you and good ol' Camp Maranatha!

Sharon Paulson
Staff Letter - 1997

Well, it's finally over. Okay, not quite. I must admit though, that I'm glad. But I really don't want to leave Camp Maranatha. I know I've been saying how badly I want to go home. I just want to get away from all the work around this place. My wish is that I could stay up here for a year or so with all my friends, I could grow so close to them and to the Lord.

I've learned a lot here this summer. I've learned about pride, about prayer, about what I really want for myself in the future. I've learned how to fix a window and a little about the drywall business (I liked that). I've even learned that I don't want to dig ditches the rest of my life. But probably the most important thing I learned was how to love those I really don't like.

If someone were to ask me what my favorite summer ever was, I would probably have to say the summer of 1986.

Mountain Top Experience

I would say this because it was the summer I learned how to be a true friend. I knew the qualities it took to be a true friend, but I unfortunately didn't possess those qualities. I can honestly say that I do now.

Robert Underwood
Staff Letter - 1986

Now that summer's coming to a close, and as I think about seeing you guys for the last time this year, I think about all the memories stored up inside. That's what makes it so difficult to write this for my last devotion.

A lot has happened to me this summer, I mean *a lot!* I think I've grown to be a stronger Christian (which I'm glad about), and because of the trials I've been through, I'll be able to endure more than ever.

As I was sitting here wondering what to tell all of you, I could picture at least a dozen times we've laughed and been silly with water fights and practical jokes. But I can also picture times we've prayed together and cried together and listened to someone when they had a problem. I can also picture a few of the fights, but we always pulled through a lot closer and stronger than we were before. That's the way it's supposed to be with a family, and I just wanted to say that I couldn't have asked for a better family this summer.

Candee Wright (Schreiner)
Staff Letter - 1986

I have come to love you guys, each and every one of you, even if at night sometimes you didn't let me sleep. You are all very special; that's something I don't want you to forget. But even more importantly, God loves you and wants to be the Lord of your lives. Just keep in mind that He is *"greater,"* but only if you let Him be.

Camp Staff

And I pray that Christ will be more and more at home in your hearts, living within you as you trust Him. May your roots go down deep into the soil of God's marvelous love, and may you be able to feel and understand, as all God's children should, how long, how wide, how deep, and how high His love really is; and to experience this love for yourselves, though it is so great that you will never see the end of it or fully know or understand it. And so at last you will be filled up with God Himself. (Ephesians 3:17–19 TLB)

Derri Knowles (Ironfield)
Staff Letter - 1988

To all of my new friends, whom I greatly love, thank you. Thank you for your entry into my life, my memories, and my eternal happiness, Thank you not only for my education and happiness, but for the education and happiness you helped provide for the Maranatha campers. Thank you for all of the good times I've had, including beating Idyllwild Pines staff in volleyball. Thank you for the Christian environment where I don't have to worry about "should I share the gospel with them?" I can see by the attitudes of your hearts and your love for God that you might know Christ better than I. Thank you for the opportunity to work here and for the opportunity to get away from my friends and family, because it made me realize how much I love them and how much they love me.

Randy Bowden
Staff Letter - 1993

For me, this summer job started on the 1994 camp work day. After that, I really started working July 20th or somewhere around that date. I spent that day working with Keith and the outside guys. I remember shoveling and raking all

Mountain Top Experience

the brush away from the shacks area with Tim (Lay) and Josh (Tate).

That night, Keith came in the guys' staff house and said, "The kitchen needs two guys to volunteer for a week." Tim and I were the two volunteers.

After two days, Tim and I liked working in the kitchen so much we volunteered for the rest of the summer.

Thus began my career in the kitchen and learning how to cook. The thing I liked most was the eating and the sleeping part of the job. That's a close tie with days off and cooking the eggs and pancakes. The only thing I really didn't like about this summer was having to eat the same food* week after week. But I really hated eating eggs every other morning, and I got tired of eating the turkey almost every other night.

Matt Krueger
Staff Letter - 1994

Note from food service: While it is true that we usually serve eggs every other breakfast, cold cereal, fruit and granola are always available as an alternative. As for the allusion to turkey almost every other night, this is a gross exaggeration. Thank you.

Well, the summer is over and it was a good one. The camp didn't burn down, and we didn't lose any campers. You guys and girls really drew together and worked hard this summer. The camp is better for it, and the people who came and met God are better for it. I hope as you go back to your routine of school or start a new routine of work, you will look back on this summer and be able to say, "God, thanks for the opportunity to serve You at Camp Maranatha."

I think next summer we will have a mock disaster and celebrate Camp Murphy* anniversary. That time really

Camp Staff

proved to draw the staff together and cause some bonding to happen.

Thanks for all the work, and thanks for working together during the hard times as well as the good.

Keith Shirley
Staff Letter - 1996

FYI: The summer of 1996 brought the "Bee Canyon Forest Fire." The camp had to be evacuated, and the staff was invited to stay at lifeguard Lynn Murphy's home in Garner Valley. Hence—Camp Murphy.

Hello, all! Unless you decide to stop reading now, you will be forced to take in one last dose of my ramblings. This letter comes with no promises and, in fact, may be harmful to your health. Proceed with extreme caution!

For those of you who are planning on coming back to be (work?) at camp for another summer, I must say, cherish it. I really noticed how much I wished I could be back once school started this year, even more so than any other year. It hit me that I couldn't just go up to anyone who was wandering around and be able to have an actual meaningful conversation like I could at camp. On the rare occasion that I found myself doing something dumb, I found that people around here looked at me like I was some freak of nature instead of blowing it off as typical Paul like y'all did this summer.

I also noticed a lot of differences when I started working at the cafeteria here at school. If you goof off too much and start soap bubble wars and so forth around here, you get more than just a stern look from Nancy. Instead, they say stuff like, "There are plenty of other people who still want to have a job here."

By the way, in honor of the guys' staff house, I have made a pledge not to try to clean my room too often (actu-

Mountain Top Experience

ally, only when I know someone new is coming over ahead of time). I haven't listened to U2 in months, because the saturation from this summer still hasn't worn off. I keep my friends from pulling money out of any fountains we happen to see, because everyone knows that you have to clean them out before it becomes legal. I refuse to watch Pocahontas because the staff guys voted against that movie by a five to zero vote. Code Red is something that no one talks about, but everyone does occasionally. I wish I had a throne like the one in the maintenance yard. I learned a lot while sitting in it. I take full advantage of the swings in the park nearby late at night (you know, before 10:00 pm). They help bring back happy thoughts as well.

Uh-oh, I just realized that this letter is starting to get a bit too serious. That means it needs to come to an end. Wouldn't want to get emotional or anything now would I, Josh, or Captain of Industry or whatever it is you are calling yourself this week? If anyone wants a copy of the "Random Thoughts" speech that I gave at the end of the summer on staff letter night, let me know and I'll send you clues on how to find it. Who knows? You may even find a certain treasure while you're digging.

Paul Hutchins
Staff Letter - 1996

In 1966, when Ralph, our oldest son, decided to work the summer in the camp, it was hard to let him go for the whole summer. But knowing the director and his wife, Errol and Juanita Hunt, we knew he was in good hands. From then on, one of our three sons (Ralph, Dwight and Keith) worked in camp for the next twelve to fourteen summers.

When Keith had his turn to work summers at camp, it became a childhood desire of his to work permanently in

Camp Staff

the camp, and he went about equipping himself for the job. Several years later, when Dick put the job opening in front of him, how could he resist? Keith readily gave up a good engineering position at Mattel (a toy manufacturer) to work at camp full time. In May of 1990, we helped him load his belongings as he again set out for camp, this time with his family (wife Paula and sons Timothy and Isaac. Daughter Larissa was not yet born).

Ruth Shirley

Is it good that this summer is over? I don't know, I have many different feelings about my time here. There were many good times and then some bad ones. There were days I didn't think I would ever leave and days I didn't want it to end.

I have grown close to the Lord. I have learned a lot about reading the Bible and about talking and telling things to the Lord. I have learned that if you ask God for something, He will usually give it to you.

I will always remember this summer with fond memories. I will probably forget the bad times and just remember what I need to know. This was a great way to spend my summer.

Jeremy Redfield
Staff Letter - 1994

I wish to thank our Lord for the opportunity to serve Him in a beautiful place such as Idyllwild. I love the job He has called me to do. I thank Him for letting me get to know all those great kids. I love them all.

Lord, I pray that they will always have You in their lives. And as long as You call me to work with kids, Lord, give me wisdom, understanding, and Your love to do so. I hope

Mountain Top Experience

I was a good witness to the kids on staff and all the campers that come through this great place.
Thanks, Father.

Janie (Hill) Hogan
Staff Letter - 1994

    This summer has been so special to me. I've had the unique opportunity to work with you all. Peace has flooded me and I have been able to face my pain and let go of it.
    I think your mission this summer has been to spread Christian joy. You all live a life that God must be very proud of. You all take all your daily little crosses in stride. And I know how hard the work has been, and you haven't complained.

Cathie (Coe) Davis
Staff Letter - 1988

Dear Nancy,
    I know our staff letters are probably not supposed to be addressed to you personally, but mine is, because what I have to say is mostly because of you.
    I feel that you most likely have a big say in who is chosen to work at camp each summer, and the young people picked this year were some of the sweetest people I have ever had the pleasure of working with. They were all willing to do anything that was asked of them, whether cleaning the camp or doing whatever was needed in the kitchen.
    And you, Nancy, have the neatest way of making everyone you talk to feel very special. You treat all the kids with respect, and they know you love them. As for me, you always let me know I was appreciated. Thank you so much for the privilege of being part of Staff 2000!

Jeannie Oleson
Staff Letter - 2000

Camp Staff

This summer started out with the normal excitement of spending time with friends and being lazy. And, as is expected, I was a little hesitant about leaving my life of sleeping in and laying around the house. Now, looking back, I laugh, thinking of how hard it will be to leave my "home" at Camp Maranatha.

As Jody (Beggs Reeves) put it in her "sermon"* that she wrote Ashly (Reeves) at Teen Camp, these mountaintop experiences are ones to remember, and, as so often happens, we shouldn't let them get lost in the valleys and deserts as we head home. It's so easy to stay close to God up here. I agree with Calvin (Jaffarian), it's like the mountain pushes you closer to Him. In the midst of the potholder skit or *My Best Friend's Wedding* soundtrack, it seems you can always feel the presence of God. So my challenge to my staff family is to keep the promises and commitments you have made and stay strong throughout the year. I love you guys.

Katie DeRoche
Staff Letter - 2000

*See "Letter to a Teen Camper" in Lessons section.

In the beginning of the summer I had a mission statement, even though it took me at least a week to write it down on paper. I had one, and it was to learn more about God and myself.

I feel that both have been fulfilled. I've met some of the most awesome and interesting people this summer. I felt blessed to work with each and every one of you. We truly had some great times, like the water fights where everyone but Tim got drenched, or the time we cleaned the boys' staff house (remember, Marco?), and the time we danced "If You Want to be Happy For the Rest of Your Life" (Calvin, you never looked better). We've had a lot of fun this sum-

Mountain Top Experience

mer, made a lot of new friends. I love you all and always keep you in prayer.

**Melissa Matthews
Staff Letter - 2000**

I would like to thank you all for allowing me to help out for a few weeks this summer. Some people take walks down memory lane, but I actually got to work on it! I got to see a lot of you guys (more of some than I would have liked—you know what I mean) this summer. You're a great group of kids with your hearts full of love for the Lord. May you continue to grow in Christ this school year, and may He bless you all greatly.

Dick, Nancy, Keith, and Paula, thanks for sharing your summer kids with me. God bless.

**Sherry (Trivitt) Christiansen
Staff Letter - 1999**

I can't believe that this summer is just about over. It's been a very busy one, but filled with a lot of fun. I was so happy when Dick asked me to work as lifeguard and cook. Whenever I come to Camp Maranatha, I am filled with such love, peace, and joy. I sit at the pool, before the campers come, and listen! I hear laughter and screams of joy, people just loving to be at a beautiful Christian camp.

Thanks to all the boys for covering and uncovering the pool and helping in the kitchen. Thanks to all you sweet, loving, joy-filled girls for all of your help in the kitchen and coming to visit me at the pool. Julie (Wilson Fogel), Sarah (Paulson Tate), Bobbi (Crawford), Jeannie (Oleson), Sherry (Trivitt Christiansen), and Shannon (Wickens Lazar), thanks for all you give in the kitchen and in everything you do. Jody (Beggs Reeves), for listening and giving me words of wisdom and the little black pills! "Ha, ha."

Camp Staff

Thanks to the Shirley family for all you give to camp and to my family. Dick, thanks for wanting me here and for all you do for me and my family. Nancy, you are awesome. What you give to us words can't express!

But the fruit of the Spirit is love, joy, peace, patience, kindness, goodness, faithfulness, gentleness, and self-control. (Galatians 5:22–23)

. . . everyone should be quick to listen, slow to speak, and slow to become angry. (James 1:19)

So in everything, do to others what you would have them do to you . . . (Matthew 7:12)

Michelle Johnson
Staff Letter - 1999

My first years at the camp, all the staff boys had nicknames given to them. I remember I had the name of Head-a-Hopper. All the newer staff members had the job of cleaning the bathrooms (you can probably guess how I got this name). I remember Jerry Davis had the name of Stinky, because he always put on cologne. I can't remember the other names, but they all had to do either with their job or their personality.

I also remember for several years having the job of being the lifeguard and having to clean the pool every day. During those days, we had the horse stables right next door to the pool, and there was always plenty of dirt and dust to clean because of the horses and rodeos they had. It was fun for awhile, but it got old as the summer wore on. Some days I couldn't face the job of vacuuming the pool. Instead, just before the campers came to swim, I would swim along the bottom and stir up the dirt so no one would see it. At other times, the pool filter would back up and all the dirt

Mountain Top Experience

would come back into the pool. What a mess! Instead of nice clear water, the pool was brown looking. That's when we had to get Errol with his special chemical treatment. Hopefully, your filters don't have this problem anymore.

I remember one time when we had a girls camp renting the grounds. Some of their camp counselors wanted us to scare the girls in their cabin that night. We dressed in dark clothes and used flashlights to shine on our faces and look scary. Little did we know their church bishop (if that's what he was called) was going to be there that evening. I don't think he knew about what was going on, because he and some of the other staff ran after us through the woods. We thought once we made it to the woods they would stop coming, but they just kept running after us. We finally made it to the rock cave behind the A-Frame and stayed there until all calmed down. Good thing they couldn't tell who we were, because the next morning all was well and back to work as usual.

Another time, on the Fourth of July, the Hunts were off the mountain and we had no rental camp on the grounds. Idyllwild was having some kind of an event, and all the motel rooms in town were full. So we (the teen staff) thought, here is a way to make some money for the camp. You guessed it, we opened the cabins for use as motel rooms, opened the snack bar, and provided the swimming pool. We had some guests and made some money, but never in our young minds did we think about the camp liability or insurance problems. All turned out well, but once again, Camp Maranatha gave us a good learning experience to build into our lives.

Ken Steinseifer

My experience at Camp Maranatha was great. Why? Because I met new people who became my friends and co-

Camp Staff

workers. The friends I'm talking about are the ones who are listening and reading this paper. I'm going to tell you what I learned this summer at Camp Maranatha. I learned how to use the meat slicer, mixer, dicer, Norman, sink, grill, and many other things. The most important thing I learned was patience. Be patient when the little kids walk up to the serving line in a bunch or when you have to kinda yell at the kid so you know what he wants, or when the small kids answer in a whisper to your question and you can barely hear them. The kitchen was work all right. It was fun for many reasons, like Sarah (Paulson Tate)'s funny songs with Lisa (Richard) and Sharon (Paulson), and the most fun of all was Brian (Reeves) and me bugging Darci (Murphy).

Camp Maranatha gave me more than friends or a job, but a second home and family. I would be glad to come back next year and be a part of Staff '97. I hope I'll see everyone there from '96, especially Josh (Tate), Paul (Hutchins), Job (Tate), Ron (Bowse), Wes (Shoemaker), Tim (Lay), Grant (Jaffarian). My story of you guys will be finished in some year, of course, but I don't know which one, so I shall mail it to you and you mail it to someone else. Good-bye and so long.

Noah Lynch
Staff Letter - 1996

Ahh, the summer. This past summer was one of the best times of my life. Being in "gifted programs" and such for most of my life, I had to spend a lot of my time with school. And in my free time I would have nowhere to go so I would loaf around at home. Needless to say, I didn't get out much. But then this summer, for the first time, I spent all day among friends, I did things! What a time we had. I had freedom I never had before. Things other people my age take for granted, like spending money on snack food,

Mountain Top Experience

or having enough money to spend on snack food. And the memories . . .

We had gone to rent a movie that night; me, Greg (Marshall), and Cynthia (Condon). After much looking around, we finally decided on *Camp Nowhere*. Part way through the movie, the VCR ate the tape. As luck would have it, we started flipping channels and found one of Greg's favorite movies just finishing up. After that, it was getting late-ish and I had to, uh, empty my bladder before bed. Well, I don't want to go into details, but it didn't go quite according to plan, because someone (actually it was more than one someone) had "gift wrapped" the toilet.

I remember long periods when we tried to beat Grant (Jaffarian) at Risk. We made alliances and tried desperate gambles and brilliant strategies, but it never happened. After a while, we all got tired of Risk and, like Monopoly before it, it became another closet space eater.

There was a time once when, by mistake I'm sure, all the guys ended up on maintenance. It was raining and our task was to cut up some logs and roll them down into the gully so they could be collected and used for firewood. Somehow, we decided (and I doubt it was my idea) to do this with our shirts off. We had a lot of fun that day.

The work was a new experience for me as well. It was the first time I was responsible for getting up and heading off to work, and in retrospect, it wasn't that bad. Learning to work in the kitchen was also new to me, but I guess it was a valuable experience. There were times I almost enjoyed just working among friends; the times they would ambush me by hiding under a bed, waiting for me to come by with the vacuum, or just talking while we cleaned cabins. It was these kinds of experiences I will probably remember the longest, and it's also these things that make me

Camp Staff

want to come back. Besides, I need to get you guys back for the toilet thing . . .

Calvin Jaffarian
Staff Letter - 1999

How do you talk of a summer of feelings? From septic tanks to the beach to just the daily meals, the summer of 1988 was special. Special people, all gathered for a special reason, make for a perfect summer. Last year had its problems, and the year before, too. But this year, a team spirit felt by everybody brought the task of running a camp down to the level of earthly, for one unearthly Master. I felt that God was in total control of this camp, that everybody let Him take control. Fighting God's will in the past has made for a slow-moving disorganized summer.

So here we are, some have already left and the others are soon to leave and go back to their families, friends, and usual lifestyle. I hope and pray that God will guide each and every one through a safe and sane life. The memories made this summer will fade a bit but never be forgotten. It takes a special type of person to spend an entire summer working for others, and God has brought the best of those people to Camp Maranatha to serve Him. With sixteen Camp Maranatha summers under my belt, I can honestly say all of these people on staff are truly my great friends.

The days have gone by, one by one, and they will continue to. So just go with the flow and let God lead the way.

Good will come to him who is generous and lends freely, who conducts his affairs with justice. Surely, he will never be shaken; a righteous man will be remembered forever. (Psalms 112:5–6)

Kevin Beggs
Staff Letter - 1988

Mountain Top Experience

Camp Maranatha holds a lifetime of memories for me. I have been a camper, summer staffer, and year-round assistant manager. I have also worked on special building projects, have been on committees that operate and make improvements to the facilities, and I have been involved with our camp programs. Taking part in so many aspects of Camp Maranatha's ministry has given me many experiences I will never forget.

Some of my fondest memories are of working on staff in my teen years. It was then that I learned to work with my hands and with people. It was also a time of great spiritual growth. I have four memories that really stick out in my mind from that period.

The first is learning to drive the camp jeep. I remember driving it down to the dairy every morning for fresh milk.

The next memory I have is setting up a triple bunk bed in our staff cabin. The monstrous bed was too tall for our cabin, but we figured out a way to solve that problem. Our floor was dirt so we dug holes for the legs until the bunk fit. The guy on the bottom bed was just a few inches from the floor and the guy on the top bed was in the rafters, but no one seemed to mind. We had the only triple bunk in camp!

Taking the big flatbed truck to the old burning dump was a once-a-week event that no staff boy wanted to miss. In addition to bringing back treasures, we had a variety of dump games. Our favorite was having a guy throw a big glass bottle up over the dump while the rest of us stood armed with bottles of our own. Once the big bottle was midair over the dump, it was our job to smash it by throwing our bottles at it.

Finally, one of our favorite after-hours things to do was to go into town to the local ice cream parlor and sing around

Camp Staff

the player piano. The owner said it brought more customers so he would occasionally give us free ice cream.
Dave Crimi

After retiring, I was offered a job at Camp Maranatha in the area of maintenance. The year was 1987 and I was 66 years old. What a privilege it was to be able to participate in a ministry in such a beautiful and natural setting and to be able to work with the dedicated leaders of the camp.
Ralph Reid

The following is a true story. One of the names has been changed, but those of you who were there are sure to know who this is about! Just remember we all love each other.

The Dust Shifter

Some of the summer staff boys were working on a project in the upper end of the camp. One of the staff girls developed an interest in this project (or perhaps in the staff boys?) and started hanging around and asking questions. After a while, the boys found her presence annoying and they tried to make her feel unwelcome, hoping she would take the hint and leave them alone. The effort was unsuccessful.

Finally, one of the boys got a bright idea. "Say, Suzie Q (not her real name)," he said, "I just thought of something that you could do to help us. Would you please go back to the maintenance building, ask Mr. Hunt for the dust shifter, and bring it to us?" Mr. Hunt, who was no dummy when it came to playing tricks, caught on to the situation very quickly. "Oh, yes," he said. "Let me think. I wonder what we did with it last time we used it." He led Suzie Q (again, not her real name) all over the maintenance area in a search for the requested item. An hour or two later, Suzie Q (you know) returned to the upper end huffing and puffing,

Mountain Top Experience

dragging behind her a large attic fan. Mr. Hunt had given the boys just what they needed.

How long did it take "Suzie Q" to catch on? Well, no one seems to remember. It may even be that she's figuring it out just now as she reads this.

Walt Shirley

Dave Crimi has many stories that he tells on Barry Tate. Even though they lived in Vermont, Barry's four sons (Joel, John, Josh, and Job) continued the Tate tradition of serving on staff. I have found them to be a pleasure to work with. Each of the boys has made an impact on summer staff and has added to our supply of Tate stories.

Joel, who often called himself "Dunderhead" during his staff experience, worked the summers of 1990 and 1994. (He and his wife, Christine, also spent June and July of 2001 as an on-site staff family. The staff kids especially enjoyed spending time with their daughters, Elisabeth, age 2, and Gracie, who celebrated her first birthday here at camp.)

Many of the memories I have of Joel's time here involve trauma to his glasses. We played a lot of volleyball, and Joel always had an enthusiastic attitude towards the game. In one game he took a shot right in the face. I tried to fix his glasses with Super Glue, which seemed to work pretty well once the glue dried and the fumes stopped making his eyes water. Another time I was showing Joel how to thread pipe. He was done threading and gave a big whirl to backspin the threader off the pipe. The pipe on the other end came up and hit him in the face, or should I say glasses. The handle flung his glasses across the shop, and we speculate that may be what broke them that time.

John worked in 1990, 1991, and 1992. John did not want to pass up his dad who worked three summers, so he didn't return to work a fourth time on staff. John did, how-

Camp Staff

ever, spend time at camp as a member of the summer ministry team. He came a few days early and worked with his brothers, Josh and Job.

I remember two stories that demonstrate John's unflagging determination (some might call it stubbornness):

John and I were calculating the volume of a tank one day. He disputed my calculation of the area of a circle—Pi times radius squared. He *knew* it was Pi times diameter squared. I showed him that diameter squared was the area of the square that the circle would fit in, but he would not accept that he was wrong. He challenged me by asking how long it had been since I studied this topic. He left that summer still thinking I was wrong and he was right. (I'm certain that maturity will one day help him see the error of his ways.)

There are several good hiking trails in the area, but most people choose just one. On their day off, John and Robert Underwood had me take them to the South Ridge trail. They hiked up to Tahquitz Peak, then to San Jacinto Peak, then to the Tram, and back to the camp. All in one day.

Josh was on staff in 1994, 1995, and 1996. He served on the 1997 summer ministry team and stayed on for an extra week to help out on summer staff. Those of you who know Josh will understand when I say that he has a unique approach to life.

One summer, he brought only one pair of work shoes with him. He wore them for everything, I think he actually wore them to church on occasion. They were in pretty bad shape by the end of summer. At one point he used Duct tape to hold them together. At summer's end, he buried them under the swings across the gully. When he returned the next summer he dug them up. During the year my son had a *Weekly Reader* that had an article on the world's most disgusting shoes contest. We were not surprised to read that the winner was from Vermont.

Mountain Top Experience

During general cleanup, it is common for the staff to find loose change left in the cabins and around the grounds. They have a contest as to who finds the most money by the end of summer. Josh saved his and buried it after each summer. Then when he came back for the next summer he would dig it up and add the next year's find. The last summer he was planning on being here, he buried it under the grate to the door of North Lodge. One other summer he buried it in Paula's flower garden. Even now, about $33.00 in charge is buried in some undisclosed location on the campgrounds.

Josh also has unique problem-solving skills. Once when we were working in the upper end, Josh had ripped holes in his pants. He had learned how to use a hammer stapler for putting felt on the roof. Josh got the brainstorm to staple his pants together. So he stuck a shovel down his pants to hammer against and started to staple. That worked for him.

Josh's love for painting was, unfortunately, not matched by his neatness. He usually got more paint on himself than the wall. His staff shirt became his uniform for such projects and at the end of summer he hung the shirt in the paint shed. It hung there for several years before it was used as a paint rag. Then again, you could say it had always been used as a paint rag.

We try to take the staff to the beach at least once each summer. We went as a group, with ice chests and all the gear necessary for a successful beach trip. Josh and Paul Hutchins spent the whole day sitting on the ice chests in their long pants and long sleeved shirts, staring at the waves. We tried everything from football to volleyball to boogie boarding, but nothing worked. There they sat, one on each ice chest, and after all that exercise you can bet we were hungry.

Camp Staff

Here at Camp Maranatha, we have the occasional dryer fire. One of these occurred as we arrived back from the airport with Josh and Job. We pulled that dryer out and I had Josh take it back to the maintenance yard. He had it on a dolly with a strap around it. Instead of taking it into the parking lot, he went up the hill in front of the dining hall. The hill was apparently too steep, got the best of him, and he stumbled. Both the dolly and the dryer fell on top of him. Janie (Hill) Hogan, our cook, came to his rescue. He survived the incident, but sustained some nasty bruises on his upper arms.

As was earlier stated, Dave Crimi often tells unflattering stories about Barry Tate. One summer, Josh and Job took it upon themselves to avenge the tarnishing of their father's good name. So the staff guys cooked up an idea to jump Dave Crimi as he was sleeping. Their plan was to tie him up and leave him in the middle of the lawn. They even got some of the staff girls to help. Dave remembers waking up in his bunk and seeing a girl. Well-acquainted with the camp rules, he yelled, "No girls allowed in guys cabins." With that, the Tate boys ran and ditched Dave in the dark. The next day, Dave was taken on by the Tate brothers on the center lawn. Job had a net and a rope to try to tie him up. There was a lot of running around and heavy breathing, but they eventually quit without accomplishing their mission.

Job was here for the 1995, 1996, and 1997 summer seasons along with working March and April of 1997. He claimed he would return in 1998 and not worry about his dad's legacy, but as of 2001, no Tate has served more than three summers.

As for Job, well, he had a little trouble replacing a window one time. I had measured the opening and given him the appropriate replacement glass, but he couldn't seem to

Mountain Top Experience

make it fit. I asked him which dimension was wrong. He replied that it was too short in height and too long in width. Without saying a word, I held up an imaginary piece of glass and rotated it ninety degrees. Problem solved.

Pictures of Job's dad (Barry Tate) and Paul's uncle (Paul McIver) going through the dishwasher inspired Job and Paul to reenact the event. With careful planning, they first removed the hot water from the machine and replaced it with cold. It was unfortunate that no one thought about the hot water that was sitting in the pipes. Once inside the dishwasher, however, Job was quick to discover the oversight and bolted from the machine in record time only slightly scalded. Now there are pictures of this second-generation dishwasher experience to sit alongside the originals. These are sure to be coveted family treasures!

Keith Shirley

Apocryphal Empiracles

So many of my memories of Camp Maranatha started out as fabrications and embellishments which over the years have developed into full-blown lies and deceptions. I'm almost positive that at least some of them are based on actual events. I just can't remember which ones. I do know that I attended Kids Kamp in the early sixties and Teen Camp in the late sixties and served on the staff for one summer in the early seventies. My staff summer was the first year that Dick and Nancy officially took over their duties.

When I worked on the staff, one of the very best chores was going to the dump. You got to ride with all the trash in the back of the old army truck all the way to the dump. Being on the trash run was a position of great respect and authority.

Camp Staff

Anyway, I do remember one trash run in particular where I got to be the center of attention, which has always been a goal of mine. I can't remember exactly who all was there, but I know for sure that Dick and David (Crimi) were and probably Dwight Shirley, Christopher Blakely, Beanie March, and Mike Shea.

The highlight of the dump run was that when you got there it was traditional for one guy to throw bottles up in the air over the dump while the other guys would throw bottles at it and try to break it. I'm sure this activity had an official name, but it escapes me now. Of course, this was all long before recycling and ecological sensitivity had become widely practiced. All I know is that it was fun to try and break the bottles.

At any rate, at one point in the middle of this contest, I saw something down in the gully that was serving as the dump that caught my attention. I decided to investigate and jumped off the truck and ran down the bank, across the dump and into the thick brush on the other side. Naturally, when those on the truck saw me down there they immediately started throwing bottles at me. Luckily, I was moving downhill and was soon out of range.

When I found the object of my desire, it proved to be not of the quality I was anticipating and I decided it was best to leave it there and retrace my path back to the truck. The bottle throwing was soon redirected in my vicinity and accuracy was improving at the same time my now uphill progress was slowing. At one point, a bottle came very close and I decided to pretend I'd been hit. I dropped to the ground with a loud scream in the midst of some thick brush, curled up in a ball and played dead. I was sure they must have been able to see me, but evidently they couldn't for, eventually, after much name calling and threats to leave, they all trooped down to search for my body. And, I know this

Mountain Top Experience

sounds odd, they never found me. I couldn't believe it. At one point, Beanie (Al March) was standing so close to me I could have grabbed his ankle. After some discussion among the searchers, the consensus was that I must have somehow sneaked down the gully and was back out on the road.

So they all hiked back up the bank, got in the truck and left. After what I judged to be a safe interlude, I made my way back up, fully expecting to see them all waiting in the parking area. I was wrong. They were gone. I was stranded at the dump. Well, camp was only three or four miles away and having no other recourse I started walking back. After a mile or so I decided I must have really fooled them. I'd won. They'd never found me. All I had to do was make it back to camp to claim victory. My only fear was that they might intercept me en route. If they caught me before I reached camp, I'd lose.

So, I pretty much stayed off the roads as much as I could, but after a while, maybe an hour, I grew more and more bold. If they hadn't caught me by then, I figured I was home free. Soon I was openly ambling down the main road big as life. Confidence was high. I'd be back by dark. By now, I was on the outskirts of town and there were more stores and houses and people and a few cars.

I wasn't paying much attention, when suddenly, coming down the street, was Dick's green Corvair. They spotted me so fast I had no time to run. The car screeched to a stop, the doors flew open and at least thirty guys piled out, raced across the street and grabbed me like I was a loaf of bread. I tried to resist, but my cause was lost. My only chance was to try to elicit aid from the several curious bystanders. "Police!" I screamed. "Help me. I'm being kidnapped. They're going to kill me!" Well, I guess no one wanted to get involved. Maybe Idyllwild didn't have any police, I don't know. What I do know is that I was in the back of that

Camp Staff

Corvair and on the way back to camp so fast I didn't even have time to file a restraining order. So I lost. And after that, when we went to the dump, I had to sit in the cab.

Jamo Jackson

Lessons

While it is true that most of us go to Camp Maranatha expecting to have a lot of fun, there is a greater purpose. All of the Bible classes and worship services and staff devotions squeezed in between swimming, snack bar, free time, and recreation have a message for us to hear, a lesson to remember long after our summer tans have faded.

Sometimes the lessons best remembered are those we learn in the toughest times, but however they are learned, we are grateful. For these lessons equip us for the road ahead. It is in this way that we grow in ability, faith, and understanding.

Mountain Top Experience

Letter to a Teen Camper:

Dear Camper,

I hope you are having another great camp experience. I remember, back in the days when I was a teen camper, having such spiritual and emotional highs. People called them mountain-top experiences. Then, in the time between camps and retreats, the promises and commitments made on the "mountain" would get lost or die in the valleys. When we were together, united in our faith and enthusiasm, we believed we would change the world for Jesus. But going our separate ways, the world too often changed us. Year after year at Camp Maranatha, we would confess to backsliding. "But this year will be different," we would say. The thing is, life is difficult.

Being a Christian is hard work. Not salvation. Salvation is a hard work that has already been completed. Salvation is God's hard work and it is finished. The hard work of being a Christian is in keeping our eyes and hearts and minds on the Lord. No matter what else surrounds us. (Even dirty dishes, grouchy parents, friends, homework . . .) When life makes us want to dance and when life makes us want to cry and when we just want to get in bed and hide under the covers, God loves us. He is there on the mountain and in the valleys.

Enjoy these mountaintop moments. They are real. And, sometimes, they will carry you through the valleys. The way your heart responds in a room full of worshipers at camp is a gift. A gift to be treasured and to remind you to worship the Lord even when your heart does not feel the sense of awe and wonder that you feel on the "mountain." For it is the Lord we worship, not the feeling. The commitments we make to Him are a work in progress. We confess to Him the intention of our will and yield to His hands to

Lessons

shape us into what He desires. "Being confident of this, that He who began a good work in you will carry it on to completion until the day of Christ Jesus" (Philippians 1:6).

I pray that you will enjoy your journey and remember these times of growth on the mountain when you go through the deserts of life. I know that God has marvelous plans for you. He will always be your strength.

I love you, Mom

It was the spring of 1984 and I was looking forward to graduating from high school. But, like so many times before, my excitement was pushed aside by a camp concern. For months I had watched my father, Dick Beggs, live in constant pain. Simple tasks were no longer simple. Sometimes, I would look up from my homework and see him outside trying to continue on with the daily maintenance of the camp while his hunched-over frame told of the terrible back pain he had been suffering. I learned so much from my dad at times like these. It's not as though he came in for dinner every night and gave us a lesson on work ethic and sacrifice. Those were things we learned from both our parents by just watching them run the camp the last fourteen years. No, it was times like these that I learned what a deep commitment Dad had to God.

People often don't understand how running a camp can be a commitment to God. I remember every summer, watching the faces of the new teenage staff members as they heard for the first time that they were scrubbing toilets for God. "God doesn't need a toilet." "True, but we don't want a filthy toilet to get in the way of God's work. The same way we don't want bad food, or indifferent service to get in the way." Imagine coming from a life-changing meeting. You're contemplating our amazing God and the changes He will make in your life. You stop at the restroom, look down and think,

Mountain Top Experience

"Gross!" You try to regain some of your wonderment only to come in to lunch on cold, soggy, grilled cheese sandwiches and a rude kitchen staff. Are you going to be thinking about God anymore? I believe that by the end of the summer most of the staff understood how important their work at the camp was.

I heard Dad come in the back door; he had picked up the mail from town.

"Any more applications?" my mom asked.

"No."

Setting up the summer staff was always difficult. There were either too many applicants or too few. This year was unusual, there were actually the right number of teenagers wanting to work at camp. The problem was that all of the guys were new. This wasn't usually a problem, because Dad would be in charge and work alongside them, but this year, he couldn't. He really needed a returning staff guy to oversee the daily work. *If only Kevin (my brother) were older*, I thought. *Or if only I were a boy, I could do it.* Then I wondered, *Why not?* Granted, I knew nothing about maintenance, and I wasn't even sure what the staff guys did all day. I had been in the kitchen, snack bar, or bathrooms for the last seven summers. But I did know how Dad wanted things done. I understood the importance of the details, and that everything we do, we do for God. I knew that whatever the job, you had to do your best, stick to it until it was done, and put everything away in the right place. Dad could trust me with the maintenance building. I had learned that everything had a place (Grandpa Beggs had helped organize everything one year when out for a visit), and that I better put things back where I got them. I had leadership ability and I was a pretty quick learner. I knew I could do it. Now, all I had to do was convince Dad. I couldn't believe it when he agreed to let me be his "head staff guy!"

Lessons

I won't pretend I was a complete success. It is very difficult to find the appropriate leadership style when you are seventeen, female, in charge of five sixteen-year-old boys and you really don't know what you are doing. I've been given several nicknames over the years, but this was the summer I earned "Little Hitler." (Obviously, I chose the wrong leadership style).

I guess I started that summer with somewhat of a chip on my shoulder. I was very unsure of how the staff guys would respond to me so I wanted to make sure they knew I was in charge (it is painful to relive the stupid times of your life, perhaps that is why my memory is so bad, now). Suffice it to say, we made our way through our working relationships. I made many, many mistakes and bad choices, but I learned so much, not only about myself and how annoying I can be, but I also learned how to change a washer in a leaky faucet, replace broken windows, and shovel like a man (it's one fluid movement, not scoop it up, rock back and forth to build momentum and them hurl the dirt forward while trying not to fall on your face or let go of the shovel). That was one of the times I could see Dad's frustration with his imperfect body. He had come down to the bowl to see how we were doing and just couldn't stand to watch me shovel so badly. He had to take the shovel and show me, and, of course, it hurt his back. I think he thought it was worth it though. He seemed much happier as he watched me try to do as he had shown me.

We all made it through that summer, and by the end I think we all felt pretty good about it. I know it wasn't the perfect solution, but I felt I had done my best to solve a problem and be a good servant. That was one of my last summers working at the camp. When I go back now I feel strangely out of place. I suppose that is what happens when you move to a new place in your life. I lived at Camp

Mountain Top Experience

Maranatha for eighteen years. Even while I was away at college, it was home. It is impossible to express what the camp means to me personally. But even more than that, Camp Maranatha is a place where God comes to live with His children. He meets them, He heals them, touches them, changes them. I feel so honored that I got to be a part of taking care of the camp. I just pray that everyone who takes part in the care, maintenance, and vision of the camp for the next fifty years remembers that first and foremost, Camp Maranatha is God's place, not ours. We are only stewards here to fulfill God's vision for the camp.

Cary (Beggs) Bursvold

Naughty, Naughty

Many of us remember meeting in the dining room, following the evening service, around the fireplace. Dear Carl and Adeline Fromhold led us in singing, sharing, talking, laughing. I can still remember the warm feeling we felt as we left to go to our rooms.

One night someone said, "What is there to eat around here?" Completely out of character, I stood up and said, "Let's go see." Several came with me. (You know who you are.)

I opened the big refrigerator door and said, "There are a few leftover hot dogs that won't be missed."

Out of nowhere came a voice, "What are you doing, Marie?"

Turning I looked into the face of our dear Juanita Hunt, director of the kitchen and dining room. My friends were gone! I don't remember saying anything. I walked out of the kitchen, out of the dining room and straight to my cabin, very chagrined.

Lessons

I was the pastor's wife of the Advent Christian Church in San Diego, but at that moment I felt like a little girl caught with my hand in the proverbial cookie jar!
Marie Drew

The following is a true story. The names have been changed to protect all parties from embarrassment. Our apologies to the horses.

The place where Camp Maranatha now sits was once used as a sawmill, and there used to be a horse trail across the property. In the early years it was not uncommon for horseback riders to wander through the camp looking for the old trail. There were also two young ladies, we'll call them Nell and Belle, who enjoyed riding their horses to the camp where they may or may not have had a close relative or two. They did this quite often, and after every visit during the summer camping season the staff boys had to clean up what the horses left behind. It didn't take long before the two boys who usually got the job, we'll call them Ned and Fred, began to resent this menial (not to mention, smelly) task. They tried to discourage the girls from riding their horses onto the campgrounds by making fun of the horses, calling them "old nags" and other uncomplimentary names. But Nell and Bell were undeterred.

Ned and Fred took pride in their achievements on the high school track team and one day added a challenge to their disparaging remarks.

"Those two horses are just a couple of old nags," said Ned.

"I'll bet I could outrun either one of them," added Fred.

That was more than the girls could take, so they accepted the challenge. Ned marked off fifty yards for the race and dragged his foot across the dirt to form a starting line and a finish line.

Mountain Top Experience

"When I say go, the race is on," he said to Fred and the girls as they got into position.

At the signal, Fred took off, but the horses didn't get the message. By the time Nell and Belle got them moving, Fred was nearly to the finish line. The girls weren't satisfied and cried "unfair" when Ned declared Fred the winner, so the boys gave them another chance. Again, the horses, apparently unfamiliar with the word "go," were left to choke on the dust of the fleet-footed Fred. The embarrassed girls trotted off with the sound of Ned and Fred's laughter ringing in their ears.

Perhaps it was just a coincidence, but after the day of the great race, two satisfied staff boys found their "load" to be much lighter.

Walt Shirley

As I sit down to write this, I find it difficult to know where to begin. You see, my position is unique. My experiences at Camp Maranatha are the experiences of my life. To express any portion of my life without mention of the camp would be to leave out the setting in which much of it took place. Even a cursory description of the physical characteristics would only serve as a backdrop to my experiences. You see, camp is more than a place to me, more than a getaway from the busy schedules of every day life, more than a place to get together with friends and catch up on the happenings of the past year. For me, Camp Maranatha is HOME. With all that in mind, I will attempt to describe what the camp, and home, means to me.

Everything I Needed to Know in Life I Learned at Camp Maranatha

In growing up at the camp, I learned everything I would need to get me through life. The campers are our custom-

Lessons

ers, so treat them with respect. Everyone is special in God's eyes. Hard work will pay off. Don't drink the pool water. Don't pee in the pool. Don't go into the kitchen unless you want to be put to work. Last one out, turn off the lights. A good sized bell can accomplish a lot of things. Don't put anything in the toilet that doesn't belong there. Don't run on the pool deck. Running down a steep incline while wearing face paint can be both exhilarating and dangerous. No job is insignificant. If you open the snack bar early, your customers will be late. If you open the snack bar late, your customers will be early. Don't drop the overhead projector. Don't drop anything unless it is really hot. Don't pick up anything really hot without hot pads. The friends you make at camp are friends for life. Clean your room. Take a shower. Creosote burns. Don't slide into second base on a dirt ball field. Football is much more fun at 6:00 A.M. and in mud or snow (if weather permits). If you don't like camp food, *tough!* Cleaning bathrooms is even less glamorous than it sounds. Last one out, lock the kitchen (sometimes even if you're not the last one out). Pranks are the best medicine. Fish line tied to a metal screen and rubbed with a wet rag makes a great sound. Plastic wrap on a toilet seat (need I say more?). A bell atop a building is too good a target to ignore. Kissing fairies do exist. Teepees are not as easy to assemble as you would think. No playing sports on the center grass. You can build anything if you have a big enough maintenance building. Just because the pool is green doesn't mean people can't be thrown into the water. Don't throw anyone into the pool (unless the lifeguard isn't looking). Stay off the pool cover. Turn off the slide water. Panda does not like Uncle David (Crimi). The A-frame roof makes a great slide with enough snow. Drive slowly. No riding your motorcycle with campers around. Horseshoes can be fun and dangerous. King snakes—good. Rattlesnakes—bad.

Mountain Top Experience

Don't eat the yellow snow. It's a long way to the tram, so don't dawdle. You need to let someone know when you leave the grounds. Staff meeting, Monday night after clean-up. Devotions are a good time for all. If the campers say no shorts, then . . . no shorts. Expect the unexpected. Have fun. Good God + Good Camp = Good Life.

To continue would be, well, boring to some and torture to most, but that is also a part of camp life. If you live at camp, it is your life. The above lessons may not help me in all aspects of life, but who cares? I'm a camp kid and my dad is the manager so I can do whatever I want.

Kevin Beggs (a.k.a. Meatball or Bam-Bam)

Staff Letters

For many years, it has been a tradition at Camp Maranatha to meet each work day for staff devotions. During this time, the staff is able to discuss the challenges that arise in the day to day operations of the camp. More importantly, this is an opportunity to remember Who we are serving and why Camp Maranatha exists. Staff members take turns leading the devotion time, sharing stories and Bible verses that encourage and inspire. At summer's end, a booklet is compiled of all the devotional material shared during the season as well as the end-of-summer Staff Letters. These letters are the final assignment given to the summer staff and are a means of expressing what the summer meant to each individual on staff. What follows is a sampling of staff letters and staff devotion material. We hope you will enjoy this sneak peak at what goes on in the hearts and minds of the camp staff.

Even though working here was a last minute decision, I think God planned for me to serve Him in this way this summer. I was pretty unsure about coming up here and living with a group of people I hardly knew. But within the

Lessons

first week I felt comfortable with everyone, and now we're like a big family. I think God used this opportunity to show me that I can live away from home and be all right. Throughout my lifetime I've been a little on the self-centered side. Working for other people has been a lesson in putting others before myself. I think the most important thing I've learned this summer is how to get along with people who are always there. It's easy to get annoyed with people when you see them everyday. Whenever this happened, I would pray to God to help me change my attitude toward that person. The next day I would always end up having to work with that person, and with a little effort I would even have fun. It seems like the summer went so fast. I've learned so much in such a short time. I've also made friends I love very much. Thank you, everyone, for making this a great summer. I'll miss you all.
**Tricia Yonemoto (English)
Staff Letter - 1988**

Once, during morning devotions, Nancy shared a saying with me. She said she picked it especially for me, and I have never forgotten it. The saying goes something like this: *When dealing with yourself, use your head; when dealing with others, use your heart.* I am able to draw on those beautiful words almost daily. What a wonderful lesson to learn.
Liz (Dobbs) Favela

I have a lot of mixed feelings about this summer. There were times I thought it would never end and times I wished it wouldn't. It's been a summer for learning and growing in both my relationship with God and my relationships with other people. I've learned to try and love people despite their faults. One of the most important things I've learned this year is that it's not up to us to judge people. God will

Mountain Top Experience

do the judging. If you judge someone, God will judge you for the same thing on judgment day.

The most important thing that's happened to me is in my relationship with God. I never used to pray. Now I try to talk to God about everything, and it's helped me a lot.

I've made some really good friends here this summer, and I know the friendships will last. When I look back on the summer, I'll remember all the good times and be thankful for the chance to be here. Thank you for all the great times.

Tricia Zimmerman
Staff Letter - 1986

Lesson of the Calculator

This acrostic was written by Nancy Beggs and given to staff members along with a Camp Maranatha calculator.

Call upon the Lord - Psalms 4:1, Romans 10:13
Ask for His guidance - Luke 9:23, James 1:5
Listen for His answer - Proverbs 3:5–6, John 10:27
Care about others - Philippians 2:3–4, Galatians 6:2
Use your gifts to glorify God -Matthew 5:16, Peter 4:10
Love unconditionally - 1 Corinthians 13
Adjust your attitude - Philippians 2:5 & 4:8
Thank Him for everything - 1 Thessalonians 5:18
Open your eyes to His wonders - Psalms 104, Psalms 119:18
Run the race with confidence - Isaiah 40:31,
1 Corinthians 9:24

Here we are at the end of our summer. I can't believe it. When I look around my room, I think I need to start packing, but I don't want to. Not only because I hate to pack,

Lessons

but, because I really did have fun. I came here thinking about how much I was going to miss my family, friends, and suffering in the 110 degree weather of a Hemet summer. But everyone up here made up for that. I had so much fun in the kitchen with all of you. We had our bad moments, but I know that when I look back I'm going to think about what a blast I had. I'll miss bringing a blanket in front of the girls' staff house and just talking. I'll miss you, Norman; we couldn't have done it without you. I'm going to go back home and miss all of you guys.

This is really a hard letter to write, cuz I feel like these are my last words to all of you. But they aren't, because even if we don't keep in touch, I know I'm gonna see you in heaven. So there are no "good-byes" here, only "see you laters." I know God has taught us all a lot this summer. He's put us through trials that we helped each other overcome. God has taught me that no matter how scared I am of something new or where I'm going, He's always gonna come with me. So now, as we move on, whether we go to a new school, a new place, or just go home, God is always with us. God promises Jesus' return, so if we don't all come back next summer, we will all be together again in heaven. And maybe God will let us cook for one of His big feasts. So now I'm going to end this letter with an "I love you" and a whole bunch of "see you laters."

Amy DeRoche
Staff Letter - 1998

When you read this I'll be gone, but I won't really be gone. I will always be with you in your hearts. At night look up into the sky at those pinpricks of light. I will be there with the other great head staff guys of the past.

In all honesty, I did enjoy working with you, most of the time. When you gave me a hug and picked on me in

Mountain Top Experience

love and encouraged me, you made it much easier for me to be so far away from home. And so, because I appreciate you all so much, I want to give you some advice about making the transition from Camp Staff back to your family, because it can be a remarkably difficult transition.

• When your mother asks you to take the trash out, the first thing you do is set up a pulley from the kitchen to the front door for conveying the trash to that point. Make a younger brother or sister clean out the trash can while you back the family car up to the front door, put the trash bag in the car, drive the car to the curb, deposit the trash there, then drive the car around the block so as to come at the garage at the right angle. Then make your younger brother or sister clean out the car while you put a new trash bag in the trash can. This is a good way to impress your parents with all you've learned from Camp Maranatha.

• Also, when eating meals with your family, if you run out of any food items on the table, like corn, perhaps, just yell, "We need more corn!" as loud as you can in the direction of the kitchen. And make a habit of jumping up at some point during the meal to say, "Oh, no! We forgot the milk!" as you scramble into the kitchen. You might keep a tin can under your chair as well.

• Come up with silly names for all your appliances and pieces of furniture, like Reginald Refrigerator and Sandy Sofa, and insist that everyone use your names.

• Put a little sign-out sheet on Reginald Refrigerator to use every time you leave the house.

• Set up a snack bar in your room and invite the neighborhood children. When they say, "If the green *Now-and-Laters* are fifteen cents and the red *Now-and-Laters* are fifteen cents, how many blue *Now-and-Laters* and *Polly Seeds* can I get with a dollar fifty-eight?" tell them three, because you can get away with that at home.

Lessons

- When using any household appliances (toasters, hair dryers, vacuum cleaners) make sure you're wearing the proper safety equipment—eye wear, ear plugs, work gloves and an apron, because your parents will be even more reluctant when it comes to workman's comp than Dick would be.

And above all else, rest up good for next summer on staff at good old Camp Maranatha.

Joel Tate
Staff Letter - 1994

One day as I lay on my bed, I noticed how much a plant can brighten up any room or give life and color to an empty spot. I thought back to the time when I didn't have a single plant in my room. I remembered how my life was brightened up by that first small plant. Since that day of discovery, I have added sixteen plants to my collection. One day I noticed that all my plants were leaning toward the window where they could feel the warmth of the sun. No matter which way I turned them, they were always struggling to be in the sunshine. I also observed that the more sunlight my plants got, the more they grew and flourished. And I thought, I wish that I, as a Christian, could be more like a plant that is always searching and struggling to find the sun. And when I find the Son, I could grow and flourish just as they do. Then maybe I, too, could brighten up somebody's life or fill an empty spot.

Holly Plummer (McCaghren)
Staff Letter - 1984

The two summers I've spent up here have helped me grow up in a lot of ways. This summer I've had to deal with a lot of anger, frustration, sorrow, and pain. I learned that I will be facing these emotions all my life, and how I cope

Mountain Top Experience

with them now will determine my happiness for the future. It's really difficult to even begin trying to understand God's plan for all of us. Thankfully, this summer provided me with friends who wanted to help me become closer with God. I've thought more about my relationship with God this summer than ever before.

The staff has taught me a lot about myself and what a true Christian is. We all had our moments, but I feel that we all know that we do love each other no matter what. Thank you for just being my friends. It means more to me than you'll ever know.

Jennifer Knott (Wagner)
Staff Letter - 1986

Another summer has passed and I've been asked to write another letter about what I've learned. I don't know how I could possibly write down on paper what I am feeling in my heart. How can I explain the lessons I have learned? Every summer and every minute that goes by, I add to the pages that go into the book of my life. And every day I realize that I would be a nobody in this crazy world without God in my life. If I have to pick something I learned this summer, it would be that in every situation and every experience I face, there is only one path that I must choose. Most of the time, I find myself wandering down the wrong road without even realizing it until Jesus comes, takes my hand, and leads me back in the right direction. I am very thankful there is a place at Camp Maranatha for people like me who can always feel they are "home" when they are there. Thank you, staff, for all your hard work this summer. You will never know how much you have meant to me!

Holly Plummer (McCaghren)
Staff Letter - 1989

Lessons

The Smallest Gift
by
Ashly Reeves
(written for staff devotions)

Once upon a time there was a farm. Now this was no ordinary e-i-e-i-o farm; this was a resort farm. In order for the farm to stay in business, the mother goose (and less widely known father goose) had to hire help from other farms. They had cows and pigs come from farms as far away as Georgia. Some came from farms just down the street. Needless to say, they were all very different animals from different backgrounds, yet with one common trait—a deep love and devotion for the Farmer. Because of this love (and all-you-can-eat worms, slop, and hay), they gave their summers to Maranatha Farm. It was the job of these ambitious barnyard creatures to make sure the guests were entertained. They put on three shows a day, and guests came from near and not-so-far to watch the show. Although the shows were fun, and sometimes performing them on time was stressful, they were always done for the enjoyment of the Farmer. Now our story finally takes place on opening night not so long ago.

"Where is chick Kashly? She said she would bring me my makeup fifteen minutes ago," said an undone Moolissa.

Then Chatty Chicken added, "I don't know, but if she doesn't show up to go over my lines with me, I'll miss the entire pasture scene."

"I'm sorry it took so long," said a small voice under the table. I was rehearsing my dance. I want the Farmer to be pleased tonight.

"Oh please, the Farmer won't even remember your stupid dance; he only came to see me. I am the best," said Chatty Chicken.

Mountain Top Experience

"Whatever," said Timmy Turtle in his thick Caribbean accent as he adoringly gazed at his strong shell in the mirror. "He will be so impressed with my massive shell, he will forget you are even on stage."

"Yeah, so get a move on, Chick, and get my tail combed." Horsey Hannah demanded.

"Well you are probably right. I am only a Chick, but maybe someday I'll be as good as Rooster Roger."

"In your dreams, little lady," crowed the rooster. "Now come rub my neck, darling."

As Chick Kashly ran around doing various tasks for everyone, she disregarded the comments of her superiors and went over her dance again and again.

Mother Goose pulled back the curtain and the show began. Fear gripped the heart of that little chick. She watched Moolissa bring the crowd to tears of laughter, then they were amazed by Timmy Turtle's shell. Chatty Chicken moved them deeply with her words, and Rooster Roger serenaded them with song. As they all finished, they looked up to the Farmer who smiled and was pleased. Chick Kashly's heart was in her throat and she panicked.

"How will I ever please the Farmer with my childish dance? It is nothing compared to the talents of the others," she thought.

It was her time to go. She, not so gracefully, headed out. The music began, so she forced her trembling knees to go on. As she weakly performed, she reached the time to do her leap. She soared through the air and landed flat on her tail feathers. She dreaded the look that must be on the Farmer's face. But when she looked up, he was smiling, urging her on. She was filled with strength and passion and had the audience standing in applause and respect by the time she had finished.

Lessons

After the show, the Farmer headed backstage, something he rarely does.

"I'm sure He's coming to give me the lead," said Chatty Chicken.

"No, He wants me to sing more songs" Rooster Roger assured them. But as He came, He walked right past their zealous faces to a figure on her hands and knees cleaning up the mess from the show. Chick Kashly's eyes locked into His as he picked her up and whispered, "Well done, thou good and faithful chicken."

Three Sisters
by
Jody Reeves

(Nancy Beggs read this on her turn to lead staff devotions)

Three sisters were swimming across a river when the current began to pull terribly and the girls were in danger of drowning. Their cries for help were heard by the sons of the king who immediately set forth upon their father's river vessel in search of the hapless damsels. Soon the three sisters were plucked from the swirling water and deposited safely upon the boat.

The eldest sister, seeing that her rescuer was a prince, thought to herself, *At last my toil is ended. I will marry this prince and never again suffer want.*

The prince, for his part, loved the girl from the first moment he saw her in distress. Soon, the two were married and his new bride wasted no time in laying her requests before him.

"Oh, my darling," she said, "I want a great, big, beautiful castle on the hill overlooking the river where first we met."

Mountain Top Experience

It was the prince's great pleasure to grant her wish, for he was a loving and generous man.

As the years went by, this eldest of the sisters would come to her husband many times a day. "Oh, my love, I need a new hat." "Sweetheart, I want a party." "I must have a new dress." Whatever her heart desired, she had only to ask and it was hers. But after twenty, thirty, even fifty years of marriage, if you were to ask her what color her husband's eyes were, she could not tell you, for she didn't know.

The second sister suffered great embarrassment that she had nearly drowned by her own foolishness. That a mighty prince had pulled her out of the river, a sopping mess, he in his fine clothes on his father's beautiful boat, made her blush with shame. But the heart of the second brother was won at first sight of the poor, bedraggled creature and they, too, were wed.

The prince loved his bride and built her a castle filled with servants to cater to her every need. He brought her to the dining hall where every evening a delicious feast was laid out upon the beautiful, ornate table. The poor girl would look upon the abundance and say to herself, *I am not worthy of such a feast, it cannot be for me.* She would then find a dark corner and sit on the floor with a crust of bread.

Whenever her husband came near, the girl would lower her head in shame and say, "Oh, please don't look upon me, for I am poor and ugly and foolish, not worthy of being rescued from the river. It was my fault for being in the river that time of year. I should have known better. I will try not to be any more trouble."

And after twenty, thirty, even fifty years of marriage, the girl could not say how tall her husband was, for she never saw past his princely boots.

The youngest sister, dragged coughing and sputtering from the raging river, looked into her rescuer's eyes and

Lessons

thought, *What a wonderful man. I must know him, if it takes me an eternity to do so.* This prince, like his brothers before him, was smitten by the girl he rescued and, before long, they were also married.

As newlyweds, they would spend hours together making plans for their castle. The young bride would sit every morning at breakfast with her husband, gazing into his piercing green eyes, listening to the rich timbre of his voice as he told her of the wonders of his father's kingdom. The two would often walk the grounds hand in hand over the terrain, rough as well as smooth. Sometimes the girl would lose her grip and fall, cutting herself on jagged rocks. But even then, she would only look up and reach for his hand. For the pain of injury was nothing compared to the joy of being with the one she loved. And after twenty, thirty, even fifty years of marriage, the girl awoke each morning in happy anticipation, wondering, *What shall I learn of my husband, today?*

How easy it is to criticize the selfishness of the first sister or scoff at the foolishness of the second girl. But how many of us can see our own prayer life reflected in their stories?

How often do I bang on heaven's door with my urgent requests? "I must have this job, this car, this answer."

At other times, I am like the second sister, overwhelmed by my own inadequacy. I focus on my poverty of spirit and do not see the glorious, rich opportunities before me.

Yet, deep in my heart, I long to be like the third sister, sitting quietly before the Bridegroom, wanting only to know Him more.

Songs & Skits

It has been said that a picture paints a thousand words, but when it comes to memories, it seems a song can paint a thousand pictures. The opening strains of a familiar song on the radio can bring to mind a particular person in a particular place on a certain day. Not only time and place are recalled, but the joy or sadness of the moment and the very smell and feel of the air. See if this is true for you. Do any of the following lyrics take you back in time to a cool summer night at Sunset Bowl? Can you see the flames of the campfire? Smell the smoke and the dust and the pines? How about some of these skits? Do you remember the excitement of preparing for the "talent" show? Did your props fail? Did you suffer from stage fright? Remember the acoustics of the Tabernacle?

We've included just a sample of some camp favorites, but we are confident that a few minutes in these pages will stir memories of many more. Go ahead and join in. Sing right out loud. No one will mind. It's camp, after all.

Mountain Top Experience

Some variation of this skit was performed at every talent show for many years. Maybe it is still being used.

A newspaper reporter stands at the edge of the stage and swings his arms back and forth as if he is getting ready to jump.

Reporter: "One, two, three—
A person dressed as a banker comes running onto the stage yelling.
Baker: Wait! Stop! What are you doing?
Reporter: I'm going to jump off this cliff.
Baker: Why would you do that?
Reporter; Well, you see, I am a reporter, and in three hours I have to turn in the best story my boss has ever read or I'm fired. I've looked all week and there is nothing to write about, so . . . *he swings his arms* . . . One, two—
Baker: No, wait!
Reporter: Nothing you say can stop me.
Baker: No. I'm not going to try to stop you.
Reporter: You're not?
Baker: No. *Starts to cry.* I'm going to join you.
Reporter: Why?
Baker: Well, you may think you have problems. I'll tell you about problems. I'm a baker, and last week I got an order to make 150 cupcakes for the governor's daughter's birthday party. I had just finished frosting the last cupcake an hour before they were due for delivery. When I opened the door to put them in my delivery van, my neighbor's cat ran into my bakery.
Reporter: That doesn't seem so bad to me.
Baker: No. It wouldn't have been so bad if the cat wasn't being chased by two German Shepherds and a Cocker Spaniel. They trampled every last one of those cupcakes,

Songs & Skits

and now I have nothing for the governor's daughter's birthday party. I'm ruined!
Reporter: *Thinks for a minute.* Well, okay. I guess there's enough room on this cliff for two of us.
Reporter and Baker: *Swinging arms.* One, two, three—
Zookeeper: *Runs onto stage* Wait! Stop! What are you doing?
Reporter and Baker: We're going to jump off this cliff.
Zookeeper: Why would you do that?
Reporter: Well, you see, I am a reporter without a story.
Baker: And I am a baker without any cupcakes.
Reporter and Baker: So . . . *they swing their arms* . . . One, two—
Zookeeper: No, wait!
Reporter and Baker: Nothing you say can stop us!
Zookeeper: No, I'm not going to try to stop you.
Reporter and Baker: You're not?
Zookeeper: No. *Starts to cry.* I'm going to join you.
Reporter and Baker: Why?
Zookeeper: Well, you may think you have problems. I'll tell you about problems. I'm a zookeeper and last night I when was feeding the monkeys I opened their cage and one of them escaped. So I slammed the cage shut as quickly as I could so none of the other monkeys could escape.
Reporter: That doesn't seem so bad to me.
Zookeeper: No it wouldn't have been if I hadn't locked myself in the cage and left the keys outside with the escaped monkey. That monkey took my keys and opened every cage in the whole zoo. By the time he opened the cage I was in, every animal had escaped. I'm ruined!
Reporter and Baker: *Think for a minute.* Well, okay. I guess there's enough room on this cliff for three of us.

Mountain Top Experience

Reporter and Baker and Zookeeper: *Swinging arms.* One, two, three—
Bride: *Runs onto stage* Wait! Stop! What are you doing?
Reporter and Baker and Zookeeper: We're going to jump off this cliff.
Bride: Why would you do that?
Reporter: Well, you see, I am a reporter without a story.
Baker: And I am a baker without any cupcakes.
Zookeeper: And I am a zookeeper without any animals.
Reporter and Baker and Zookeeper: So . . . *they swing their arms* . . . One, two—
Bride: No, wait!
Reporter and Baker and Zookeeper: Nothing you say can stop us!
Bride: No, I'm not going to try to stop you.
Reporter and Baker and Zookeeper: You're not?
Bride: No. *Starts to cry.* I'm going to join you.
Reporter and Baker and Zookeeper: Why?
Bride: *Looks at her wedding gown. Looks at the trio on the cliff.* What do you think?
Reporter and Baker and Zookeeper: You're a bride without a groom?
Bride: You guessed it.
Reporter and Baker and Zookeeper: *Think for a minute.* Well, okay. I guess there's enough room on this cliff for four of us.
Reporter and Baker and Zookeeper and Bride: *Swinging arms.* One, two, three—
Baker, Zookeeper, and Bride jump off the cliff. The reporter stands there looking over the edge. He straightens up, pulls a note pad and pen from his pocket.
Reporter: Wow! What a story!

Songs & Skits

I remember singing crazy camp songs like "Pharaoh, Pharaoh," "Madalena Catalina," and "Fried Ham." I also remember tender times around the campfire learning worship songs like "My Peace I Give to You," and "I Want To Know You, Lord." I especially enjoyed that.
Carolyn (Schenk) Gillogly

I remember skits that made me laugh until I cried!
Debbie (Drew) Miller

Here is a song from one of the talent shows entitled "Mr. Bubble." I believe it was performed by Jody Beggs Reeves, Dini (Diana) Walters McGregor, and myself. If there were others, I've forgotten. (One often blocks out the most embarrassing moments of life.) I'm sure it was Jody's idea*— Miss Creativity. She has always been good with words, songs, etc. I do remember the song and the way we dressed. We had towels wrapped around our hair and towels wrapped around our bodies. I prayed that my towel would not fall off! The song went something like this:

chorus:
Bubble, bubble, bubble, bubble,
Bubble, bubble, bubble, bubble

Mr. Bubble in your tub'll
Make you squeaky clean
Pour it in the water
Turns it pretty green.
Mr. Bubble, suds, suds, suds
Mr. Bubble, suds, suds, suds
Oh, Mr. Bubble, Really gonna suds tonight.

Mountain Top Experience

chorus

If you're going on a date
And you want to smell great
Buy some Mr. Bubble
And don't be late.
Mr. Bubble, suds, suds, suds
Mr. Bubble, suds, suds, suds
Oh, Mr. Bubble, Really gonna suds tonight.

I've never been more embarrassed in my life.
Jeanette (Schenk) Henneberry
*Editor's note: I happen to know that Jody (Beggs) Reeves, clever as she is, did not write this song. I believe it was from a television commercial advertising bubble bath.

One skit we did at the campfire was of Moses. Mike Tapley laid down behind the wall in back of the campfire and raised his feet and legs up and said, "Moses, these are the feet of God. They move like this when I am not busy (slowly) and like this when l am busy (fast). Right now I am busy so I need your help . . ." At one point Dave Tapley (Moses) threw down Rod Sherry as his rod. Between my grandparents and camp, I think my humor is very warped.
Ellen Koehler

The graces sung before meals* are still sung today. And I cannot hear "Amazing Grace" without breaking into the chorus in Navajo . . . *Ah Yo An Te* (sp?). "How Great Thou Art." Thank you, Cameron Ainsworth! Truly God is amazing.
Debbie (Peckens) Hammond
*Editor's note: Remember this one?
"For health and strength and daily food we give Thee thanks, O Lord." (sung in a round)

Songs & Skits

My favorite parts of camp were the talent shows. Since I was very little, I always looked forward to them. One year, I think my grandma (Lillian Koehler) would have preferred Beth (my sister) and me not be involved. We got up in front of everyone and sang a song my grandpa taught us about a black crow doing his business in a country store. That was one of my grandma's favorite stories to tell. Every time she told it, her body would shake with laughter and tears would roll down her face.
Gwen (Koehler) Marron

I remember talent shows with goofy skits and songs.
Carol (Peckens) Laroche

Rah, Rah, Potatoes and Ham

This famous staff talent show number was first presented in the 1970s and continues to be sung to sooth hungry campers when waiting for more food to be brought to the serving line. For talent shows, it is often performed with pot holder choreography.

Rah, rah, potatoes and ham,
Yum, yum for pancakes and Spam,
With our ovens cooking fast,
We'll bring your dinner out at last.

When to the pool you may go,
Our lifeguard's watching, you know,
When you drown she'll drag you out,
After an hour you did shout.

Our snackbar's open for you,
Selling you candy and other goo,
When your stomach's feeling sick,
To our clean bathrooms rush real quick

Mountain Top Experience

We always clean up your mess,
For you we all do our best,
We're the Maranatha crew
And we're here to work for you.

Who Are the People in Your Campground?

The words to this familiar tune were changed and performed by the staff as a talent show number. Jennifer (Knott) Wagner and Jody (Beggs) Reeves were responsible for most of the lyrics as we recall.

Verse One:
We're in the kitchen all day long,
Cooking things to make you strong;
If you should get a stomachache,
Don't blame it on the food we make.
The servers will serve your food,
Always in a happy mood,
They'll slop it right on your plate,
And never ever make you wait.

Chorus:
Oh the cooks* are people in your campground,
In your campground, in your campground.
And the servers* are people in your campground.
They're the people that you meet
When you're walking down the street,
They're the people that you meet each day.

Verse Two:
The dishwasher will scrub your plate,
Cleaning up what you just ate;
He puts them in his nice machine,
When they come out they're sparkling clean,

Songs & Skits

The bathroom cleaners work each day,
Scrubbing all the germs away,
They work so hard the whole day through,
To get the bathrooms clean for you.

Chorus

Verse Three:
The lifeguard works out in the sun,
Watching over everyone,
If you are drowning you just shout,
And pretty soon she'll pull you out.
The snackbar is a happy place,
Where you can really stuff your face,
And we will serve you speedily,
For Christy is our boss, you see.

Chorus

If you have got a broken bed,
Or water dripping on your head,
Our maintenance guys are what you need,
They'll fix it for you, yes indeed.
The manager's a busy man,
He'll try to help you if he can,
But when it's time for you to pay,
You're sure to find him right away.

Verse Four:
The camp director is so rad,
As long as you are never bad,
So just be good and you will find,
That you will have a real swell time.

Mountain Top Experience

The camp nurse is the one to see,
If you should ever scrape your knee;
She'll wash away the dirt and grime,
And fix you up in record time.

Chorus

Verse Five:
If you are feeling kind of blue,
Your counselor's always there for you;
Though sometimes they might seem real mean,
If you don't keep your cabin clean.
The campers are a sloppy bunch,
You should see them eat their lunch;
They throw their food both here and there,
They even got some in my hair.

Chorus

These words in the chorus change to fit the people mentioned in each verse.

Most of the skits I remember are visual pranks, like "measuring for a coffin" and "guessing their weight." Both of these get the unsuspecting victim wet.

Sheldon Koehler

Here are some of Sheldon's favorite silly and not-so-silly campfire songs:

On Top of Spaghetti
Here We Sit (Like Birds in the Wilderness)
The Grand Old Captain Kirk *(Tune: "A-Hunting We Will Go")*

Songs & Skits

Announcements:
Announcements, announcements, announcements,
A terrible death to die, a terrible death to die,
A terrible death to be talked to death,
A terrible death to die.

Clementine
Do Your Ears Hang Low?

I Points to Myself (*As you sing this action-song, point to the proper body part when you mention it. For example, point to the top of your head when you sing Topnotcher. Continue singing and add another part of your body for each verse and repeat the others going backwards in reverse order. Try as many verses as you want. For the boom-boom, clap hands, bang tables, or stamp your feet.*)

My Bonnie Lies Over the Ocean—(*This one is fun when participants change from sitting to standing and vice versa with every "B" word in the chorus and first verse.*)

The Worms Crawl In
Kum Ba Yah

Taps—(*Sung around the flagpole in the evenings as the flag is lowered. Sometimes accompanied by trumpet, cornet, or bugle.*)
Day is done, gone the sun,
From the lake, from the hills, from the sky;
All is well, safely rest, God is nigh.

Mountain Top Experience

Who remembers these camp standards?
Don't Chuck Your Muck In My Dustpan/Red Wagon/Fish and Chips and Vinegar/One Lollipop
You're in a Putt-Putt

How did Moses cross the Red Sea?
How did Moses cross the Red Sea?
How did Moses cross the Red Sea?
How did Moses cross the Red Sea?
How did he get across?

Did he walk? No, no.
Did he run? No, no.
Did he fly? No, no, no, no.
Did he jump? No, no.
Did he swim? No, no.
How did he get across?
God blew with his wind puff, puff, puff, puff
He blew just enough, nuff, nuff, nuff, nuff.
And through the sea God made a path.
That's how he got across.

I've Been Redeemed
It Only Takes a Spark
I'm Bringing Home My Baby Bumble Bee
Give Me Oil in My Lamp
Do Lord
I Am A C-H-R-I-S-T-I-A-N
Get Your Elbows Off the Table

Songs & Skits

I Wish There Was a Kingdom
[Words and music by Jane Gransee (Mergens) and Cary Beggs (Bursvold) – ages 7 and 8?]

Chorus:
I wish there was a kingdom,
that had real golden streets,
And you could fly all over,
and never put down your feet.

Verse One:
My friend, your wish is answered,
I know the place it's at,
For I have been there also,
and I will never come back.

Chorus

Verse Two:
The place it is called heaven,
if you be good you'll go there
If you don't, you'll go to Satan,
and you will burn down there.

Chorus

Verse Three:
My friend you must be careful,
this is my warning now,
So just believe in Jesus
and He will show you how.

Mountain Top Experience

He's Everything To Me

[this original second verse was written by Jeanette Schenk (Henneberry) and Jody Beggs (Reeves) during a junior high P.E. class]

If you're lost and lonely just like me,
And you need someone to help you see,
He's the answer; He will set you free!
Jesus is the key.

After all, for you He gave His life;
He'll lift your burdens and He'll ease your strife,
Just believe and He will give you life
For eternity.

For that great day will be coming soon,
And all earthly things will come to ruin;
Tell your friends that there is lots of room
For anyone who dares
To meet the God that cares,
And love and laughter will fill the air.
It's the end of darkness and despair,
And I pray that I will see you there;
You're everything to Him.

One teen retreat, I remember sitting in the A-Frame next to Robby Osborn. As we all sang "For Those Tears I Died," I understood in a new way, the love of Jesus for each one of us—a love so very great that He died to rescue us from our pain. I was overcome by this love so personal, so self-sacrificing, and so present. Robby kept looking at me as *my* tears began to flow. I was only fourteen and a bit self-conscious, wondering what he must be thinking of me, until he told me he wished he could cry like that.

Songs & Skits

I think about Robby even now when I sing that song and I pray, wherever he is, that the seeds planted in his heart during those teen retreats and Teen Camp experiences will always remind him of the great love Jesus has for him. When he is hurting, or when any of us are hurting, we need only remember the One who died for our tears.

Jody (Beggs) Reeves

Nature

At Maranatha, you can sit out by yourself on a rock and be completely at peace with the world.

- Paul Hutchins

Mountain Top Experience

One of my Camp Maranatha memories involves a trip that my Sunday school class from the Valley church took one weekend. Frank Depew was our Sunday school leader at the time, and we had decided to go and help build a rock dam in the gully. I remember well the time we spent working. I also remember the walks at night that all of us took around the grounds. It was always neat to me that we had the camp to ourselves. I had never been to Camp Maranatha when there wasn't some type of organized camping experience, and I think this made us all feel special. The most amazing thing about the walks was looking up at the sky and seeing all the stars. Even better was the fact that our leader was an expert stargazer and could point out the constellations and planets that were visible in that night-time sky. I always think back fondly to that one short weekend and all the kids that used to be in my Sunday school class, Tim (DuFour), Robert (Underwood), Sandy (?), Leann (Stansbury), Renee (?), Mark (Smith), but most especially, Mr. Frank.

When I worked at camp a few years after that, I had this one rock I would go to at night that I would lie back on and gaze at the stars. I spent that time talking to God, but I also spent that time remembering how Frank taught the wonders of the sky. I just wish he were still around today for me to let him know how much all he did as a Sunday school teacher has stuck with me. Most of all, I wish I could listen one more time to him tell of the wonder of that night sky and how marvelous a creator God really is.

Candee (Wright) Schreiner

Nature

I remember a night when we hiked to a spot that overlooked the valley. I went away by myself and sat alone in such a great world, but felt not so alone at all because I was one of His.
Roxanna (Tate) Sieber

I remember singing, "How Great Thou Art," and always feeling closer to God in the beautiful mountain setting.
Debbie (Drew) Miller

I have heard it said that the most memorable times in our lives are ones that were spent outdoors. Our senses are stimulated in ways that being inside can't compete with. I must agree. I don't think I will ever forget walks to inspiration point, crossing the gully to swing on the swings, hay rides on cold winter nights, swimming in the cool clear water of the pool, playing 6:00 A.M. football on a frosty morning in the ball field, sitting on a rough rock contemplating my life, tossing snowballs, making human pyramids with friends climbing on top of each other and wrestling on the grass, playing volleyball with all I had to give.

When I go to visit Camp Maranatha and I start the drive up the mountain, my heart does a little hop, skip, and jump. I have so many, many memories connected with Idyllwild and camp that my mind goes wild on the drive up. Then, when I open my car door and breathe in the sweet, unique smell, I am often overwhelmed with joy. This truly is God's country. This place is anointed with the peace and the will of God. You can feel it in the air. You can see it in the people.
Liz (Dobbs) Favela

I believe one of the most beautiful sights at Camp Maranatha was last February when we had the Conference

Mountain Top Experience

Annual Meeting up here. The day was crowned by snow—white, gentle snowflakes. Thank You, God, for this campground.
Jeannie Davis

I miss the scents, the squirrels, and the taste of the water. The first thing on my agenda, every time I went to camp, was a trip to the drinking fountain. How good it was to sing around the campfire or hike to Tahquitz Peak (I still have my "Squirrel Cards"). Boy, those were the Good Old Days!
Cindy (Howard) Bailey

When I sit alone in the Gazebo to relax, I always enjoy the opportunities to view the beautiful scenery of God's creation and to watch the birds and squirrels move around on the campgrounds.
Anna Mae Gardner

I loved singing at the campfires while looking up at the stars.
Ellen Koehler

I remember staff meetings on top of the mountain under uncountable stars.
Carol (Peckens) Laroche

The most magical times were the bonfires at night, watching mesmerized as the flames flickered up into the stars, gazing across the gully to the dark but intriguing forests beyond, singing some favorite campfire songs like, "Pass It On."
Rob Hopper

Nature

We are told we cannot always keep the "Mountain Top Experience," but I wholeheartedly disagree. God is there with us, and I always remember the first time I read the poem, "Footprints," at camp. That is how I remember. All these years later, I still close my eyes and remember walking along and smelling the fresh air and pine trees. God made these! And God allows us to remember. Psalm 34:8 tells us, "O taste and see the Lord is good; How blessed is the man who takes refuge in Him!" (NASB). I tasted the Mountain Top and I still cherish it.

Sheldon Koehler

When the Drew family arrived in California to pastor the San Diego Church, one who greeted us fondly was Chuck Anderson. He couldn't wait to show us Camp Maranatha. Our children were two, three, and eight. About the fourth week after our arrival, he invited us to spend the day. We were to leave early Monday morning, but we awoke to pouring rain. I couldn't imagine a worse day to spend at a camp with three little children. I called Chuck and suggested perhaps another day would be better.

"Oh, no, we will run out of the rain in no time," he said. So we dressed for the weather and off we went. We took two cars. After a couple of hours, we came to a sign that read, "No Further Without Chains." I said, "We can't go, we have no chains." Following Chuck, we parked in an area where several were putting on chains. Undaunted, here came Chuck with chains for our car!

We started up the mountain climb, scared, not knowing where we were going. Soon we realized it was snowing and everything was covered; it was fairyland. The children were wide-eyed and so excited as we drove into Camp Maranatha. We had a day in the snow, picnic lunch in the old Two-Story, and sledding on sleds provided by the Hunts.

Mountain Top Experience

Chuck achieved his goal, and we truly enjoyed a winter wonderland.

Marie A. Drew

    Mountain weather can be a bit unpredictable. One beautiful, clear morning seemed ideal for pouring the slab for the addition on my camp residence. John Tate, John Almon, and I gathered the materials and started mixing concrete. By lunchtime, clouds had blown in and it was raining cats and dogs. We finished up wearing waterlogged trash bags, not only soaked, but battered by hail.

Keith Shirley

Impact

*Camp is often a place of revelation and decision.
Here in the clean mountain air,
far from the distractions and demands of home,
foundations are laid,
courses are set,
commitments are made.*

*Whether it is truth taught in a way that never leaves us,
a demonstration of love that eternally touches us,
or a ceremonial swimming pool immersion that forever cleanses us,
we are affected in ways that mold our character and ultimately inspire us
to be more like Jesus.*

Mountain Top Experience

It was the summer of 1973 that I drove up the mountain for the first time on my way to Camp Maranatha. I was about to begin a new experience that would forever change my life. Just a few short months prior to my trip up the mountain, I had embraced the Christian faith and accepted Jesus Christ as my Lord and Savior. Pastor Jim Smith, and his wife Fern, were instrumental in leading me to Christ. After years of alcohol and drug abuse, my newfound faith provided me with some much needed direction for my life. I recognized early on in my walk with Christ the importance of fellowship with other Christians. Eager to move away from past relationships and disappointments, I decided that the best way to get a fresh start would be to go work on staff at Camp Maranatha. What a wonderful experience.

I was the first to arrive on staff that summer. Dick and Nancy made me feel right at home the moment I stepped foot on the camp property. I remember getting to work right away. One of my first jobs that summer was to help Dick prepare the cabins for summer usage. Little did I know that during the course of the winter someone had broken into a few cabins located on the upper end of the property to avoid cold weather. Although the water supply had been cut off to avoid pipes freezing during the winter, our uninvited guests weren't shy about using the toilet facilities. My job was to clean things up! Dick promptly nicknamed me "Scoop" and made it his summer mission to tell everyone how I came up with my unusual nickname. It was an interesting summer to say the least!

My summer at Camp Maranatha was a major turning point in my life. I had the opportunity to live with a group of young people that shared the same faith in Christ. They became good friends and helped me transition from my past difficulties of drugs, alcohol, and gang activity to a

Impact

brighter future in fellowship with other Christians. That summer I began to understand the importance of what Paul wrote in Galatians 2:20 when he said, *"I have been crucified with Christ and I no longer live, but Christ lives in me. The life I live in the body, I live by faith in the Son of God, who loved me and gave Himself for me."*

I left Camp Maranatha with a sense of gratitude for all God had blessed me with that summer. I had made up my mind that summer that God was calling me as a living sacrifice for His glory. I felt confident my future would be working with youth in a camp situation similar to Camp Maranatha. I ended up attending a Christian college in Tennessee that Fall to begin preparations for my future. Upon graduation in 1977 I accepted the position at a camp in Brazil, South America. My ministry goal was about to be realized.

As I look back on my experience at Camp Maranatha, I realize God had opened the door for me to work on staff that summer so as to begin preparing me for future ministry opportunities. He planted a seed in my heart for young people that continues to grow, even today. Dick and Nancy were wonderful examples as dedicated leaders in ministry. They were an inspiration to all of us that had the privilege of being part of their staff. For me personally, Camp Maranatha was a *fresh start to a new beginning!*

David M. "Scoop" Nelson

Camp Maranatha means so much to me for all the good times, laughs, and for all the friendships that have lasted over thirty years. Most especially for the friends we were able to turn to for prayer for my family and Seth (my son) during his twenty-two-month fight with cancer and continuing prayer!

Kathy (Hahn) Bottom
AKA "Chicken"

Mountain Top Experience

As I watch my son struggle to recite the "verse of the week" for his preschool group at church, I cannot help but think of Camp Maranatha. At age four, I didn't even know what a verse was, much less who Jesus was, or what He did for us many years ago. I am from a family that did not attend church and believed that children should make up their own minds about God.

This is what Camp Maranatha means to me. I had the privilege and blessing to be a fourth kid to Dick and Nancy Beggs. My sister, Cyndi (Walters Sapwell), and I grew up playing at Camp Maranatha, bugging the staff when they came every summer, playing hide and seek in the cabins, A-Frame, Ponderosa, and Dining Hall. We crawled through drain pipes, climbed to "Dead Man's Cave," played in the granite hills behind what is now the staff lodge, and ate countless Pop-Tarts on weekends.

Our family moved from Idyllwild when I was twelve years old. I returned to work on staff at sixteen years. This is when I truly came to know Jesus, and my life was changed forever. The best memories I have are from the years on staff at Camp Maranatha. I was baptized in the camp pool, and I learned to live, share, and grow with a lot of fun and special people.

Dini (Walters) McGregor

Year after year my grandma, Lillian Koehler, took me and other children, from church or wherever, to camp. In the sixth grade I accepted Christ as my Savior in the cabin late at night with my counselor. I believe God started to move and work in my life right from that moment. But the next summer of 1976, I had to make sure as I answered the altar call and felt the power of God's presence. I have been a dedicated Christian ever since, seeking to serve God. Serving God has led me on many adventures involving camp,

Impact

from being a camper to counselor and ministry team member.

At camp I grew from being an extremely shy little girl into a person who now gives staff development presentations. I am thankful for my spiritual home, the place I began to learn how God works showing love in our lives through community. I am thankful for the friends such as Darlene (Rigney) who impacted my life. My prayer is that Camp Maranatha will continue to be a place where people meet God and each other.

Ellen Koehler

Has camp affected our lives mentally, physically and spiritually? You bet it has, in too many ways to enumerate, and we are still privileged to attend Family Camps, retreats, Little Chief award ceremonies, etc. We are always growing spiritually from generation to generation.

Ruth Shirley

I grew up in a mostly white community, and, except for television, had no exposure to "people of color" until I attended camp. I had no problem befriending Cedro Rolands III, from one of the Los Angeles area churches, because, like the song says, "Red and yellow, black and white, we're all precious in His sight." I was glad to be able to form an inter-racial friendship at a time in California's history that was full of racial tension and unrest.

There are those who may suggest that the children of each successive generation are more rebellious than the previous; that could very well be true. There may have been times when camp administration and staff wondered if they were making a positive impact on the kids who went to camp. It is important for them to know that everyone responsible for making Camp Maranatha happen contributed

Mountain Top Experience

to the raising up of children "in the way they should go, so God's ways will not depart from them" (Proverbs 22:6). Many seeds were planted, and the sowers may not have known what would eventually grow from those seeds. But I think heaven will be populated with, not only many Maranatha campers, but others whose lives were subsequently impacted by those campers. At camp I learned to love God and His creation and to love my many neighbors who attended camp with me all those years.

Kevin Castleman

Camp Maranatha evokes the strongest of feelings within me. I have had my highest highs, my happiest moments I can remember, and a few of my lowest lows.

How can this be, you ask? Allow me to explain. I attended camp at age eleven. For me, along with countless other campers, it was my very first time away from home. This in itself caused extreme anxiety and fear. It was a time of growth. And growth is often painful. Emotions run very high for young teens and pre-teens. At that tender age, we have not yet learned how to deal with our feelings, and they often run away wild and deep. That is why I say I have experienced some of my deepest lows at Camp Maranatha. Sometimes I was lonely. Sometimes I was scared. Sometimes I was insanely jealous. Sometimes I was just plain homesick. But right along with those feelings came times of great joy for me.

As years passed, and I attended Teen Camp and weekend retreats regularly, I knew I wanted to work on summer camp staff to become a real part of Camp Maranatha. I dreamed of it. I prayed for it. And for two glorious summers, I was one of the chosen few who got to call themselves staff. Again, it was the first time I had been away from home for this length of time, and I was constantly

Impact

finding myself in trouble. It wasn't that I meant to get into trouble; it just seemed to fall in my lap, and I somehow allowed it to happen. Many staff meetings were called on my behalf because I had goofed up in my decision making, again. But Dick and Nancy were patient with me. Eventually, I grew up enough to realize what was expected of me and what I shouldn't do. I thank God for their sensitivity and guidance to this day. The daily devotions and meetings we shared helped to create the foundation of my faith. The role models I had while at camp still come into my mind regularly.

If I am feeling a little spiritually dry, a quick visit to camp will always bring Jesus back into the main focus where He should be. I believe that is why so many people flock to camp. We all feel the love of God there. His presence is clear and so easy to find.

A few of my favorite highlights of camp, that may be remembered by some, would be the hikes to the tram. These strenuous trips drew on our physical strength as well as our emotional strength and endurance. And the joy of seeing that tram at the top was immense.

Camp Maranatha brings out the strongest memories for me. Thirty years of memories packed full of joy and growth. I thank God for Camp Maranatha and especially for all the people who help make it available so others can experience some of the wonders I have.

Lives are changed and improved at Camp Maranatha. I know mine was. I'll just bet that yours was, too.

Liz (Dobbs) Favela

In 1969, as a recent widow, I attended Kids Kamp, Teen Camp, and Family Camp. I helped out wherever I could, and the directors let me stay, I think because they pitied me. I don't remember anyone asking for money. It sure was

Mountain Top Experience

a blessing to me and I was baptized in the swimming pool by Gerald Aulis at age twenty-one, when I was eight months pregnant.

Pastor Aulis also performed the ceremony in 1970 when I was married to Chuck Bailey (we've now been married for 31 years!). Chuck and I have gone to young married retreats at Camp Maranatha. All three of my children, Heidi, Leah, and Micah, have also had the opportunity to be campers. Over the years, we have lived in Idaho, Northern California, Nevada, Guam, England, and Idaho. Whenever we were close enough, I attended camp. It always seemed like a homecoming to me, a stable place in my nomadic life. In 1995 we moved to Tennessee and regret that we nor are two grandsons are able to come to camp.

I sure miss Camp Maranatha. I loved spending time in the Mission Cottage (Ponderosa) and Two-Story House and knowing my beloved grandmother, whom Dan Judy told me he considered a saint, had spent time there. I remember her laboriously walking in her walker to the Tabernacle. She and my grandfather, Paul Mansfield, were wonderful Christian people.

I am almost afraid to go back to Maranatha now. I think it would not be the same without The Two-Story House, and I doubt if anyone I remember would be there. Except the Shirleys and the Beggs, of course! I phoned Sherrill (Shoemaker Brauer), my old Kids Kamp cabin-mate, just before she died. It was a blessing to get to speak to her once more. Of course, I do plan to see her again some day. God bless you all, and please never miss an opportunity to go to Maranatha. I wish I could go.

Cindy (Howard) Bailey

My experiences at Camp Maranatha, as well as my involvement with the Valley Advent Christian Church and

Impact

my connection with the Advent Christian denomination have had a great impact on my life. My roots as a Christian were established through the Advent Christian Church and my camping experiences. The time spent as a teen at camps and rallies helped build my spiritual foundation. Growing up in the church, I felt loved and welcomed—like I was part of a large family. There were always smiles, warm greetings, and hugs. Many of the people I came in contact with have left an indelible impression on me. I appreciate the time that was spent nurturing and teaching me.

My first employment was at Camp Maranatha. I learned responsibility and about team work. Dick and Nancy Beggs were wonderful role models for me. Their dedication to the camp, the ministry of Jesus Christ, the way they treated me, and the example of their marriage have all made an impact on my life. Their influence did not end when I left camp. Nancy has been a spiritual advisor for me many times throughout the years.

My experiences at Camp Maranatha mean a great deal to me. One of the things I hoped for my children was that they would have similar experiences. Being involved in the Christian Church (Disciples of Christ) has made that possible. My girls have attended church camp every year since they finished fourth grade. My oldest daughter, Sara, has served two years on our area Youth Ministry Council and has been involved in the planning and implementing of high school rallies and camps.

I, too, am involved in the camping ministry in our area. I have served as a camp counselor at three camps during the last two summers, and as a sponsor at several of our high school rallies. I will return again this year as a counselor. I am also serving on our area Camp and Conference Committee. My hope is that the youth and children I come in contact with leave camp with the knowledge that they

Mountain Top Experience

have been loved, nurtured, and have heard the message of Jesus Christ like I did at Camp Maranatha.

My involvement at Camp Maranatha, and with the Advent Christian Church, has significantly impacted my life in my eventual calling into the ministry. I have been called to work with children and youth, and I have no doubt that my calling is a result of the love and care I received as a youth.

Carol (Peckens) Laroche

My experiences at Camp Maranatha have had an impact on my character, career, and continuing involvement with Christian camping.

- Working on the summer staff in 1967, '68, and '69 exposed me to the Christian role models of Errol and Juanita Hunt, Dick and Nancy Beggs, Dave Crimi, Olga Mellor, and others. This built on the foundation laid at home to give me strength of character in following Christ.
- The opportunity to operate some heavy equipment and do some construction helped guide me into my career as an agricultural engineer with John Deere.
- I have been active in working with our own camp in Iowa because of the heart for Christian camping that developed in my years at Maranatha.

Ralph ("Ralf") Shirley

Time seems to fly by and memories are made before there's a chance to plan for them! Certainly this summer has a plethora of memories I won't soon be forgetting. Thankfully, though summer's fading, I have all those memories of you all's faces, smiles, comments, nerf guns, etc, to fall back upon.

Impact

I wish I had more time to have shared more with each of you. I suppose, however, looking back to this last summer, there's one memory that I pray, despite age, trial, and test, I'll cling to undyingly. It's simply the memory of a question I found myself pondering endlessly: What is it I love more, the passions of the world, myself, or my Savior?* For some reason the Lord took me by the shoulders and made Himself undeniably real this last summer. And all the memories that I didn't have time to plan for have become joyfully a part of this other world of mine out here in the Midwest, changing me dramatically. You all are a part of that, and each of you I genuinely care for deeply. It's my prayer that all of us will be taught daily how to love our Lord more deeply and to have yet an even more passionate desire to serve Him!

Thanks again for everything you guys have done. This last summer has truly been one that's changed my life. It was absolutely unbelievable to spend time with my cousins, Tim, Isaac, and Larissa, in May. I miss you all deeply. I feel like my life's kind of getting started now, school's almost done and I have a life to start living. I praise the Lord for the opportunity I've had to spend time with family that I might not have the chance to do in the future! Thank you guys!!

Grant Jaffarian
Staff Letter - 1999

*Editor's note: Grant shared with us at devotions and also spoke at Family Camp about his pondering of the question mentioned above. I was particularly struck by his assertion that mankind's purpose for being is essentially to give glory to God. This thought stuck with me day after day during my thirty-minute commute to Camp Maranatha. On one trip, words came to me in a song which can be found in "Poet's Corner."

Mountain Top Experience

I have been thinking about camp and the good times we had. I wish we still lived in California just so my sons could experience the impact that I have experienced from Camp Maranatha.
Al "Beanie" March

Camp Maranatha has had a major influence in my life. Over the years, I have attended Family Camp, Kids Kamp, and Teen Camp in Idyllwild. I always looked forward to spending my summers there, and have enjoyed the friendship and the awesome faith-building that goes on at camp.
Christina (Parker) Gilbert

Dear Dick and Nancy,
Thank you for having me on staff this summer. I've enjoyed working up here. You gave me the chance to grow spiritually by letting me come up. If I were at home, I probably would still not have accepted Jesus as my Savior.
Brian Wade
Staff Letter - 1988

Summer Christian camping has always been meaningful to me, having attended Camp Nooksack in Washington every summer during my youth and early marriage since I was about thirteen, and, of course, my experiences at Camp Maranatha. Being "away from it all" in a Christian environment had a significant impact on my life and helped shape my character, as did Aurora College.
Judy (Hall) Menish

As I've reflected on the many experiences I've had at Camp Maranatha and thought about the way they have shaped my life, I have realized that the people I've had the privilege of working with have had, and continue to have,

Impact

the biggest impact on me. I am so thankful for the opportunity the Lord has given me to work with so many dear Christian brothers and sisters.

Dave Crimi

The summer I worked on staff at Camp Maranatha truly became a rite of passage into adulthood for me. As many who worked on staff that summer will remember, the beginning of our summer was unlike any other. Our team hike up the mountain and subsequent ride down the Palm Springs Tram turned tragic when a piece of the braking system came loose and fell through the roof of our gondola, killing a woman right before our eyes.

I will never forget the mixed emotions I felt as we descended into Palm Springs. I felt angry that something as horrific as this could happen. I was deeply saddened, because I knew in my heart the woman was dying in front of me. But I was also relieved that she was not a close friend or a member of my group. I struggled all summer with the guilt caused by my feelings of relief, but feel I became a stronger person for having gone through the experience. I have no true way of knowing this, but I feel I would not have found the positive lessons of witnessing that accident if I had been with any other group of people.

The staff that summer, both teen and adult, truly helped me learn positive lessons, as well as acknowledge the negative that a traumatic experience like that can bring to any individual. By living with the group who had witnessed the same accident that took the life of a stranger, and working through all the strange ways our emotions about the accident came up over the summer, I became a better, stronger person for having gone through the experience. I hope that my poem* about that summer helps others through their life experiences and helps them learn all the lessons, both

Mountain Top Experience

good and difficult, that we are challenged with as we continue to grow as caring human beings in this world.

Susan Reimenschneider

Editor's note: You can see Susan's poem in "Poet's Corner."

Camp Maranatha was special in so many ways to me. It was where I experienced a lot of firsts. Mainly, it embodies the foundation my faith was built on. It also carries with it so many happy memories of my family and church family. Camp, for me, was an essential part of how I was raised and who I became.

I think camp was just plain fun. There was hardly a dull moment, and just when there was a lull in the excitement, the pool would open and we would go and wear out the favorite boys' counselor by jumping all over him. Hey, there's two more firsts for me. The first time I went down a pool slide and the first time I swam under water while holding my breath.

At camp we learned crafts, games, sports, and we met friends. Some people may think that is all we got out of camp, that we forget about the lessons we learned about God, the hours we spent in classes, and the other lessons we learned about life. It isn't until later when we realize all that camp meant—what we really got out of it.

Gwen (Koehler) Marron

I've met some of my closest friends at camp, and I know that without Camp Maranatha I wouldn't be where I am today in my walk with Jesus. I've grown so much, and, like many others, I accepted Jesus at Camp Maranatha. To this day, every time we drive up Maranatha Drive, I get butterflies in my stomach just thinking of all the memories made there and how many more will be created with every visit.

Melissa Matthews

Impact

One of the most rewarding parts of working at the camp was to see the love and sincerity of the personnel in helping shape the spiritual lives of those attending the camp. This was not only of benefit to the attendees, but also had a real impact on my personal growth. The daily outside devotions were something I really looked forward to.
Ralph Reid

Last summer, during a thirty-day stay in the hospital, I received a Camp Maranatha bear and T-shirt. I hung the bear over my bed in the hospital room. All the time I was there, these gifts reminded me of the many good times I experienced and enjoyed at Kids Kamp, Work Camp and the Youth Retreat. These thoughts helped get through some of those long days in the hospital. More than twenty-five years have gone by since the accident that confined me to my bed has kept me from visiting the camp, but the memories and the caring prayers of people from Camp Maranatha continue. Thank you.
Victor Wright

I wish everyone could have the experience of working at Camp Maranatha because it sure had many fond memories for me, and many close friendships were made that will never be forgotten.
Ken Steinseifer

I can't remember a summer in my childhood years when I didn't spend at least a week at Camp Maranatha. From first attending Family Camp with my parents (Tom and Sara Cruce) to being old enough to attend Kids Kamp, and then finally moving on to Teen Camp, summer meant time for camp! My family moved a great deal as I was growing up, and that made camp all the more special for me. While I

Mountain Top Experience

often adjusted to new towns, schools, and churches, Camp Maranatha was a constant. I always looked forward to the dear, familiar faces I would see during those long-awaited weeks in the summer and weekend retreats during the school year.

Camp Maranatha had a tremendous impact on my spiritual growth as a young person. Camp is where many of my closest life-long friendships were established, friendships deeply rooted in our love for the Lord. While I didn't accept Jesus into my heart initially at camp, it is where I learned how to live out my commitment to Christ as a teenager. Both as a Teen Camper and a Kids Kamp counselor, camp was the training ground for a life devoted to the Lord. Directors Darlene Rigney and Jack DuFour, along with camp speakers like Scott Linscott and Barry Tate, left indelible impressions on my life through their godly direction, insights, and influence during those years.

Katie (Cruce) Kelly

The best part of my third summer on staff was that I met Jennifer (Knott) Wagner. Since the summer of '85, we have been friends and have shared the best moments of our lives together. Many thanks to Camp Maranatha for bringing me one of my best friends!

Patty Rabell-Moreau

I first came to Camp Maranatha the summer of '84 for Teen Camp with a group from the North Park Community Church. The following summer, thanks to the support and encouragement of Dave Crimi, I began working there at the age of fifteen. (At the time, it wasn't usual to hire anyone under sixteen, but how could they refuse Dave's recommendation?) I believe I worked three summers, and an occasional winter retreat when needed. I will always

Impact

remember Camp Maranatha as being some of the best times of my life. The friendships made during those years are truly eternal, although in this lifetime we are separated by time and distance. One day soon, there will be a great reunion in heaven where we will all see each other again.

Derri (Knowles) Ironfield

I was exposed to many wonderful saints of the Lord up there at camp, and I have many fond memories of God's people gathering for the various camps and activities. I feel very blessed and fortunate to have had the experiences. My wife, Margaret, and I continue to support the work of camp Maranatha and continue to keep Dick & Nancy and the camp staff in our prayers.

John Connelly

Bertha Cassidy was traveling through California on her way home to Canada after many years as a missionary to China. It was the late '50s and I was a twelve-year-old Teen Camper when I had the privilege of meeting Miss Cassidy at Camp Maranatha. Sitting on the bunk beds in one of the cabins, I sat spellbound with several other young girls as she told of her exciting adventures, and explained the most important job in the world—winning souls to Jesus Christ. We had a special camp memory book that year, it had a cover that looked like wood with open spaces for autographs and study notes. I cherished for years the note from Bertha Cassidy and the passage she wrote in my book that became my life verse: "Being confident of this, that He who began a good work in you will carry it on to completion until the day of Christ Jesus" (Philippians 1:6).

I spent my junior high and high school years convinced that I, too, would go to a foreign field as a missionary. It became a sort of protection for me as I also began to notice

Mountain Top Experience

boys and dream of being a good Christian wife. I was quick to tell any potential date that I was "going to be a missionary." Not every boy was thrilled to hear that. But I wasn't ashamed to say that I had made a commitment to Christ at camp and was expecting His direction in my life. It was also at Teen Camp that Pastor Les Mark (then the pastor of the Tustin Advent Christian Church and later a missionary to Mexico) encouraged us to begin to pray for God's choice of a spouse for ourselves. I took that message to heart and began praying in earnest.

It was at Camp Maranatha that I first heard about Aurora College and began to hear of students making plans to go back to Illinois after high school graduation. Aurora seemed like an extension of camp, and I wanted to go there! It wasn't "When are you going to college?" It was "When are you going to Aurora?" The transition to college was made easier for me by the camp friends who went there with me and who had preceded me: Nancy (Crimi) Beggs, Steve Lay, Janet (Fletcher) White, Glenn Schmekel, Cliff Anderson, Tim Gustafson, Barry Tate and Kay (Mooneyham) McGath, to name a few.

After two years at Aurora, this California girl returned to finish college at Cal State Fullerton. It was there that I met the man I had been praying for since that lesson at camp, Tom Cruce. After determining that Tom was "The One," I knew one of the first places I wanted him to see was Camp Maranatha. Camp was part of me and had impacted my life in such a profound way that I felt Tom would know me better if he could experience camp too.

Oh, about becoming a missionary? I've discovered through the years that one doesn't need to go to China or Africa to be one of God's missionaries. You can be a missionary wherever you are. I'm grateful for the many opportunities God has given me to serve Him over the years

Impact

after my spiritual roots were established at Camp Maranatha. My present mission field is on the Internet where I am in charge of a twenty-four-hour chat room for Christian crisis counseling. As an employee of the Crystal Cathedral, I train and supervise volunteer counselors serving from their home computers in twenty-three of the United States and three foreign countries. Bertha Cassidy was right. The most important job in the world is helping people find Jesus!

Sara (Summers) Cruce

Conclusion

At the end of the day, the very last day, there will be no packing of suitcases, no last-minute picking up trash, or tearful good-byes. When, at last, it is time to go home, we will not take a trip down the mountain, back to the lowlands. We will not carefully shelter the fragile spark ignited in our hearts with the hope that it will spread to other hearts before it can flicker and fade. No, we will not go down; we will not go back. We will not clutch our memories close—those memories that served to remind us of a higher place.

On the last day, the very last day, we will not say good-bye. We will say,
Hello.
At last, we are Home.

Mountain Top Experience

THE FOLLOWING NAMES ARE LISTED ON THE DARLENE RIGNEY MEMORIAL GAZEBO FOR THEIR CONTRIBUTIONS OF SERVICE TO THE DEVELOPMENT OF THE MINISTRY OF CAMP MARANATHA:

Frank Anderson, Sue Beardsley, Avis & Ronald Bezanson, Adlai & Katherine Bowden, Sherrill Shoemaker Brauer, Clarence & Eleanor Campbell, Roy Connelly, Will Cooper, Tom Cruce, George Depew, Lori Strauss Dill, Sim & Leota Draper, Rev. Elwell (Rick) Drew, Rev. Paul & Hope Friedmann, Carl & Adeline Fromhold, Gladys Gandy, Steve Glen, Robert & Margaret Glover, Errol Hunt, Ruby & Edward Jaffarian, Elizabeth Knechtel, Lillian Koehler, Clark Lay, Aleta Lobb, Ken Mellor, Floyd & Edith Mushrush, Harry Pitts, John Reed, Darlene Rigney, Al & Betty Schmeckel, Ethel Schmeckel, Frank Scott, Earl Shoemaker, Yvonne Shoemaker, Phil Shuman, Harold & Bertha Taylor, Vernon Woodgate

**"THE MEMORY OF THE RIGHTEOUS WILL BE A BLESSING . . ."
PROVERBS 10:7**

In Honor

THIS QUIET PLACE FOR PRAYER AND MEDITATION WAS BUILT BY FRIENDS OF DARLENE MARIE RIGNEY, 1960-1993, IN FOND MEMORY OF HER UNSELFISH SERVICE AS ADVENT CHRISTIAN CONFERENCE YOUTH DIRECTOR AND TO HONOR MANY OTHERS WHO SERVED THE LORD IN THE DEVELOPMENT AND MINISTRY OF CAMP MARANATHA.

Mountain Top Experience

Donations toward the cost of *Mountain Top Experience* have been given in honor of the following people:

GERRY AND ALICE AULIS

Gerry and Alice Aulis have been active supporters and participants at Camp Maranatha for many years. Gerry, former pastor of the Tustin and Pasadena Advent Christian churches, has been involved in the construction of several of the structures at camp, and helped, most recently, with the beds for New Big Pine Lodge. Both of the Aulises have participated in our conference camps and retreats. (Remember Chief Nikomas interpreting Chief Thunderbird's Bible stories in front of the campfire at Kids Kamp?)

Carol (Aulis) Muska

BRAD AND INA BEGGS

In the '70s, our first ten years here at Camp Maranatha, Mom and Dad Beggs would come visit us for a month or so. Dad would always ask for things to do. Some of these jobs were building small items, organizing the maintenance building, and fixing whatever needed to be fixed. On one of these trips he noticed the uneven roof line on the staff house and the "Taylor Cottage" (now Keith and Paula Shirley's residence). He designed and built the porch roof as you see them now. Mom would walk the grounds picking up trash and straightening benches, etc. She often found coins and would turn them in to the camp treasury. It was a joy for us for Mom and Dad to be part of our new ministry, even for just visits. Dad was very talented in all aspects of building and repairs, and I'm grateful he passed that on to me. Thank you, Mom and Dad, for sharing in the ministry of Camp Maranatha.

Dick and Nancy Beggs

In Honor

DICK AND NANCY BEGGS

Many of the contributions made to Camp Maranatha by Dick and Nancy are well known. However, we, their children, have a unique perspective on the ministry of this special couple. At one of their first Christian Camping International Conventions, those involved in camp ministry were cautioned not to neglect their ministry to their families. Our parents took this to heart, and we believe it is not only reflected in their marriage and in our lives, but also in the "personality" of Camp Maranatha. A common theme among those who have experienced the camp, whether as campers, leaders, or staff, is that it is a place where relationships come before policies. We thank God for laying this foundation from the beginning, and we thank our parents for serving in such a way that has not left us feeling resentful of their ministry. We are proud to be camp kids and grateful for parents who seek to serve the Lord in their work *and* in their home.

Jody Reeves, Cary Bursvold, Kevin Beggs

LEROY CONNELLY

My father worked tirelessly for many, many years on the Camp Management Committee. Dad was one to see a need and work to get it accomplished. I know he and my mother, Hazel, felt led by the Lord and contributed many hours and many dollars to further the Lord's work in this beautiful camp setting.

My recollection is that Roy was active on the management committee in some capacity or another from 1951 right up until his death in 1988 at age seventy-seven. He had a keen interest in seeing camp succeed and steadily worked toward that goal.

John Connelly

Mountain Top Experience

BOB AND BETTY CRIMI

First in Carlsbad and then at Camp Maranatha, Bob and Betty Crimi have been a part of the Southern California Conference Camping program since its inception. Over the years, they have been involved with every aspect of camping. They have set up tents, planted flowers, taught crafts to Kids Kampers, counseled Teen Campers, led workshops at Family Camp, washed pots and pans, set tables, cleaned bathrooms, painted, mixed cement, served in leadership roles in the conference and on various camp committees. They have been an encouragement and support to all of the full- and part-time staff over the years. Most recently, they have become the liaisons between the local thrift shop and Camp Maranatha, providing much-needed items, such as curtains, sheets, bedspreads, highchairs, strollers, microwaves, and crock pots at very reasonable prices. Also, it is not unusual these days to find them at the camp working alongside one or more of their children, grandchildren, or great-grandchildren. We are so grateful they passed on their love for the camping ministry to all of us.

Dick and Nancy Beggs; Dave and Jody Crimi; Gene and Cole Crimi; Joe, Jody, Brian, and Ashly Reeves; Jim, Cary, and Danika Bursvold; Kevin and Allison Beggs

TOM CRUCE

Tom's love for the Lord and his earnest desire to serve Him were clearly evident in several of our Advent Christian Churches extending over a period of many years. Few laymen have had the impact and influence that can be attributed to Tom during his forty-nine years of life. Tom had a superb ability to relate to all people in a kind and considerate manner. In addition, he enthusiastically used his gifts in service to the Lord at Camp Maranatha. He served as director of Family Camp with a creative Olympic theme to

In Honor

coincide with the 1984 Olympic Games, and, among other things, produced the Conference Life Newsletter for a time. He is well-remembered for his example of cheerful, productive service to Christ and His church.

Sara (Summers) Cruce and Katie (Cruce) Kelly

GEORGE DEPEW

George Depew is remembered for his help in putting the cement deck around the original camp pool. (Mona tells us, "Some unlucky young man lost his wheelbarrow of cement into the swimming pool." perhaps that is how we came to have a shallow end?) George was also active in assisting Betty Crimi with craft supplies, and both of George and Mona's daughters, Pauline and Christine, served as counselors at Kids Kamp. Former Kids Kampers may remember the years George brought his telescope to camp and gave them a glimpse of God's heavens. They called him Chief Moonshine.

Mona Depew

ARLENE DOUGLASS

In memory of Jack's Mom for her loving example of a godly woman who gave of herself to those around her. She will be truly missed.

Jack and Marilyn DuFour

ELWELL "RICK" MASON DREW

With Rick's deep appreciation for the beauty of nature and his love of Native American culture, Camp Maranatha seemed to him the ideal setting for Christian fellowship. For many years in the early days of Kids Kamp, Rick served as Chief Golden Eagle (Big Chief). Rick and Marie's three children (Sheri, Debbie, and Mike) and their two California grandchildren also attended Kids Kamp. In 1979, Rick

Mountain Top Experience

and Marie moved to Hemet at the base of the hills leading up to Idyllwild, a stretch of road that had always held a special place in their hearts, because it meant they were nearing their beloved Maranatha. While in Hemet, Rick stayed active in the Lord's work, serving ten years as the Conference President of the Southern California Advent Christian Conference, twelve years as a chaplain for Hemet Hospice, five years as the Hospice Chaplain Coordinator, and four years on the board of directors for Hemet's Prime of Life program. Rick fondly remembered his time at Maranatha. In his own words from his final summer at Kids Kamp in 1969, "The fellowship, food, fun, and friendships found here at Camp Maranatha will remain forever with us!"

Rick is affectionately remembered by his wife Marie, their three children, eight grandchildren, and two great-grandchildren. The fellowship, food, fun, and friendships we shared with Rick will remain forever with *us*!

Rob Hopper

LILLIAN KOEHLER

My grandma took us to Bonita Avenue Church every Sunday. She took us to Family Camp every summer and sent us to Kids Kamp and Teen Camp every year, the retreats, too. Sometimes we would whine and cry about going, but every year when she would come to pick us up from camp we didn't want to go home. She set the building blocks, which would later become our faith, in her life I think that was the greatest gift she gave me. My faith is the way it is today because of what I learned in these places.

Ellen Koehler

In Honor

DARLENE RIGNEY

Darlene was my favorite counselor. She was always so patient with us (and we gave her many reasons to exercise her patience!). Darlene was an example of Christian love and character and has affected the lives of many. Though her life was short, her ministry continues in those, like me, who experienced the love of Christ through this remarkable woman.

Carolyn (Schenk) Gillogly

About Our Contributors

Thanks to the following writers and illustrators who shared their stories, time, and talent in the making of this book.

Almon, Janet - Janet attended Kids Kamp, Teen Camp, Teen Retreats, and Family Camp growing up. In the past few years, she has been a counselor and had a variety of leadership roles at each of these camps. She has also worked on staff for short periods of time when she has been able to. She is attending Lancaster Bible College in PA, but lives with her family in Spring Valley, CA, when she is home from school.

Bailey, Cindy (Howard) - Cindy participated in Kids Kamp, Teen Camp, and Family Camp. She and her husband, Chuck, live in LaVergne, Tennessee.

Beggs, Dick and Nancy (Crimi) - Nancy attended Kids Kamp, Teen Camp, and Family Camp with her parents, Bob and Betty Crimi, and brothers, Dave and Gene. She participated in camps both as a camper and as a counselor. She later married Dick, who has been serving as camp manager/director since 1970. Their children Jody (37), Cary (35), and Kevin (30) grew up on the grounds of Camp Maranatha.

Beggs, Kevin - Kevin's entire childhood was spent as a resident of Camp Maranatha. He has participated as a camper, counselor, and staff member. He lives in Temecula, California with his wife, Allison, who is expecting their first child in May, 2002.

Bottom, Kathy (Haun) - Also known as "Rooster" or "Chicken" (thanks to her fellow summer staffers). Kathy and husband, Chuck, live in Long Beach with their

Mountain Top Experience

daughter, Becky, and her husband. They are looking forward to the arrival of their first grandchild. We pray that God will continue to comfort Kathy and her family in the recent loss of her son, Seth.

Bowden, Randy - Randy worked on summer staff. He and his wife, Julie live in Apple Valley, California.

Bursvold, Cary - Cary, second daughter of Dick and Nancy Beggs, called Camp Maranatha home from the age of three until she was graduated from California Lutheran University. She was involved in camp as a camper, counselor, and staff member. She lives with her husband, Jim, and daughter, Danika (age 2) in Vista, California.

Caron, Saundra [Reynolds] - Saundra happily worked in the kitchen for short periods of time over a couple of summers. Saundra lives in Bend, Oregon. Her children, Matthew (25) and Rebecca (22) also live in Bend, and daughter Sarah (20) lives in Gresham, Oregon.

Castleman, Kevin - Kevin attended Kids Camp and Teen Camp. He and wife, Tonya, live in Anaheim, California, with daughter, Kristin (16), and son, Kevin (13).

Christiansen, Sherry (Trivitt) - Sherry has been a Kids Kamper, a Teen Camper, teen summer staff member, Kids Kamp counselor, Teen Camp counselor, and the craft lady for Kids Kamp and Teen Camp many times. Her daughter, Meghan, has also served on staff, and Sherry has helped out when needed in recent summers. She lives in Saugus, California, with her husband, Gary, and their children, Meghan (17), and Tyler (20).

Connelly, John Sr. - John has attended all the camps over the years since camp opened in 1951! He and wife of 25 years, Margaret, are retired and now live in Temecula, California. Grown children include: John Jr. (Big Bear City); Jodi (Upland); and Jill (Fallbrook).

About Our Contributors

Craig, Abby - Abby has attended Camp Dunamis, one of our summer guest camps, as a camper and as a counselor.

Crimi, Bob - Bob and his wife, Betty, met as campers at Carlsbad, before the purchase of the Camp Maranatha property. Bob served on the original camp board and he and Betty, along with their children, Nancy (too old to tell), Dave (him too), Gene (ditto), have participated in Family Camp, Kids Kamp, and Teen Camp. For more on their camp involvement, see "In Honor" section. Bob and Betty live in Idyllwild.

Crimi, Dave and Jody - Dave has been actively involved in the ministry of Camp Maranatha from the time his parents (Bob and Betty Crimi) brought him to camp as a child. He and his wife, Jody, live in Encinitas, California, and currently serve as co-directors of Teen Camps and Retreats. Dave is also the current President of the Advent Christian Conference of Southern California.

Crimi, Gene - Gene, youngest son of Bob and Betty Crimi, was a Kids Kamper, Teen Camper, and Family Camper. He and his son, Cole (13) live in Ventura, California.

Cruce, Sara (Summers) - Sara was a Kids Kamper, Teen Camper, Kids Kamp and Teen Camp counselor, and Family Camper with husband, Tom, and daughter, Katie. Sara presently lives in Anaheim, CA, close enough to hear the fireworks from Disneyland every night. She works at the Crystal Cathedral in Garden Grove, California, where she oversees a team of volunteer counselors with New Hope Crisis Counseling on the Internet.

Davis, Cathie (Coe) - Cathie served as an adult summer staffer in 1988. Her children, Christy (28), Josh (26), Genny (20), and Sean (11), have been to Kids Kamp and Teen Camp, as well as volunteering time in the camp kitchen. Cathie, Dave (her husband), and Sean live in Idyllwild.

Mountain Top Experience

Davis, Jeannie - Jeannie lives in LaVerne, California, with her husband Otis. They have two children, Charles and Mary. The Davis family has attended work weekends and have provided the children's program at Family Camp for twenty-five years.

DeRoche, Amy - Amy is the oldest child of Joe and Pam DeRoche, who worked on summer staff in 1980. Amy has attended Kids Kamp and Teen Camp and served on summer staff in 1997, along with sister, Tauna. She lives in Hemet, California, with her parents, brother David (11), and sisters Katie (16), and Halie (10). (Sister, Tauna, is attending Biola University.)

DeRoche, Katie - Katie is the younger sister of Amy DeRoche and shares the same family ties. She has also attended Kids Kamp and Teen Camp as a camper as well as serving as Chief Nakiki at Kids Kamp 1999, 2000, and 2001. Katie and her best friend, Ashly Reeves (granddaughter of Dick and Nancy Beggs), have worked on staff in the summer and on weekends. Katie lives in Hemet with her family.

Drew, Rick and Marie - Rick and Marie have been involved in Kids Kamp, Teen Camp, and Family Camp in a variety of ways. Their children, Sheri (Freeman), Debbie (Miller), and Mike also participated in camp events. Marie lives in Hemet, California. Rick was nearly eighty-five when he died in January 2000.

English, Tricia (Yonemoto) - Tricia and her sister, Susie, served on summer staff at the ages of sixteen and fifteen. She attended Kids Kamp and her whole family went to Family Camp. She lives in Canoga Park, California, with her husband, Michael.

Favela, Alvaro and Liz (Dobbs) - Liz attended Teen Camp (Nancy Beggs was a counselor, pregnant with her son, Kevin). She never missed a Teen Camp or retreat from age

About Our Contributors

eleven to eighteen. She served two summers on staff. Liz and Alvaro live in Sylmar, California, with their two children, Joshua (5), and Lissa (2).

Froehlich, Bonnie (Pitts) - Bonnie was a Teen Camper, counselor, and served two summers on staff as lifeguard in '59 and '60. She and husband Keith have lived in Idyllwild, California, for the past twenty years. They have two grown children, Michael and Tedd, and two grandsons, Nick (4), and Cole (18 mo.).

Gardner, Anna Mae - Anna Mae has attended camps at Maranatha since she was a little girl. Her brother, Tom, served on summer staff and now lives in Texas. Anna Mae lives in San Diego with her mother, Pat.

Gilbert, Christina (Parker) - Christina and her husband Micah attended Kids Kamp and Teen Camp, and have both served as counselors at Kids' Kamp. Micah also worked on summer staff. They live in Denver, Colorado, with their son, Donovan (born September 2000), and their second child is due January 15, 2002.

Gillogly, Carolyn (Schenk) - Carolyn attended Teen Camp and served as a counselor at Kids Kamp. She and her husband, Adrian, live in Nashville, Tennessee, with their sons, Austin (8) and Aaron (6).

Hammond, Debbie (Peckens) - Debbie has been a camper at Teen Camp and Family Camp. She served as a counselor at Kids Kamp and Teen Camp, as well as working on summer staff. Debbie and her husband, Bob, live in Douglasville, Georgia. They have four children; Lisa (28), Erin (26), Melissa (23), and Scott (20).

Hardi, Dean - Dean served on summer staff in 1975 and now lives in Camarillo, California with his wife, Rhonda, and their children, Jessica (9), and Jacob (7).

Hay, Laura - Laura and her husband, Steve, served on the staff of Kings Kamp for several years before becoming directors. They live in Long Beach, California.

Mountain Top Experience

Henneberry, Jeanette (Schenk) - Jeanette lives in Decatur, Illinois, with her husband, Kirk, and their children, Joel (13), Kayla (10), and Natalie (9). Jeanette attended Kids Kamp, Teen Camp and teen retreats, and, as an Idyllwild resident, sometimes helped in the camp kitchen on weekends. She is the sister of Carolyn (Schenk) Gillogly who is also a contributor to this book.

Hogan, Janie (Hill) - Janie worked on summer staff as a teen and later as an adult alongside her own teenagers, Celena and Christina. Janie lives with her daughters and three grandchildren in North Hollywood, California

Hopper, Rob - "Robby" attended Kid's Kamp from 1977 to 1980 and Teen Kamp in 1981. He now lives in Santee, California.

Hutchins, Leslie (McIver) - Leslie attended Family Camp, Kids Kamp, and Teen Camp. She and her husband, Steve, live in Alhambra, California. They have three children; Paul (25), Bradley (22), and Amy (13).

Hutchins, Paul - Paul served on summer staff. He and his wife, Cyndi, live in Whittier, CA.

Ironfield, Derri (Knowles) - Derri first came to Camp Maranatha in 1984 with a group of teens from North Park Community Church. She applied for a staff position and was hired the next summer (though not yet sixteen years old), enjoying it enough to work the following two summers, as well. She lives in La Mesa, California, with her husband, Mike, and their son, Jared, who will celebrate his second birthday this year.

Jackson, Jamo - Jamo attended camp as a child and worked on summer staff. He lives in Fallbrook, California.

Jaffarian, Calvin - Calvin is a nephew of Paula (Jaffarian) Shirley. He served two seasons on summer staff and lives in Richmond, Virginia.

About Our Contributors

Jaffarian, Grant - Grant Jaffarian, Paula (Jaffarian) Shirley's nephew, worked on summer staff. He lives in Naperville, IL.

Jaffarian, Jeff - Jeff attended Family Camp with his children for several years. He has seven children and twelve grandchildren. Jeff and his wife, Natalie, live in New Zealand.

Johnson, Michelle - Michelle is our current lifeguard at Camp Maranatha and also serves as a cook. She lives in Idyllwild with her husband, Brian, sons Christopher (18) and Conrad (14), and daughters Chenay (12) and Kayla (9). All of her children have attended camp.

Kelly, Katie (Cruce) - Katie attended Family Camp, Kids Kamp, and Teen Camp. She also counseled at both Kids and Teen Camp. She and her husband, Greg, live in Alpine, California.

Koehler, Ellen - Ellen has been involved in almost every aspect of camp life, starting as a camper in 1973, and, after growing too old for Kids Kamp and Teen Camp as a camper, continuing to be regularly involved as a counselor and summer ministry team member through 1996. She lives in Riverside, California.

Koehler, Sheldon - Sheldon has attended Kids Camp, Teen Camp, and Family Camp. He has served as a camp counselor and a camp board member. He resides in Port Angeles, Washington, with his wife Elizabeth and their sons, Avery (5) and Stuart (1).

Krueger, Matt - Matt worked on summer staff and now serves our country in the armed forces.

Laroche, Carol (Peckens) - Carol was a Teen Camper, Kids Kamp counselor, and served three summers on staff. She and husband, Matt, live in The Woodlands, Texas, with daughters, Sara (18), Emma (16), and Julia (13).

Mountain Top Experience

Lynch, Noah - Noah has been a Teen Camper and has served as a counselor and summer staff member. He lives in National City, California.

March, Al "Beanie" - Beanie was a camper and summer staffer. He lives in Athol, Idaho.

Marron, Gwen (Koehler) "Rena" - Gwen attended Kids Kamp, Teen Camp, and Family Camp and served on summer staff. She and her husband, Shaun, are expecting their first child in April of 2002. They live in Foothill Ranch, California.

Matthews, Melissa - Melissa's great-grandparents, Errol and Juanita Hunt, served as the first managers for Camp Maranatha. She has attended Kids Kamp, Teen Camp, and teen retreats and worked on summer staff. Melissa lives in Wildomar with her parents, Chuck and Robin, and sisters Jessica, (who has also served on summer staff), Rachel, Rebecca, and brother, Daniel—who have all attended Kids Kamp.

McCahgren, Holly (Plummer) - Holly was a school friend of Cary Beggs and worked on summer staff as a teen and as an adult. Her husband, Scott, is the grandson of Errol and Juanita Hunt, the first managers of Camp Maranatha. Scott and Holly live in Mesa, Arizona, and have six children: Nicole (19), Robert (18), Shawna (16), Chris (10), Lindsay (8), and Erica (5).

McGregor, Diana (Walters) - "Dini" befriended the manager's daughter, Jody, as a first-grader. As an Idyllwild resident, she spent much of her childhood on the grounds of Maranatha. She attended Kids Kamp, Teen Camp, and Family Camp and returned from her new home in Hawaii to serve as a teen on the summer staff. Dini now lives in Snohomish, Washington, with her husband, Mike, and their children Danny (5), Katie (3), and Ryan (1).

About Our Contributors

McIver, Marilyn - Marilyn was a Family Camper. She is the mother of Leslie (Hutchins), Paul, and Robin. She and her husband, Wallace, live in Alhambra, CA.

Menish, Judy (Hall) - Judy served on summer staff in 1960. She has raised three children, Janita, Christopher, and Kamela and happily plays grandmother to her five grandchildren, in addition to husband Joe's five grandchildren. She and Joe make their home in Washington and Arizona and plan to travel throughout the United States by motor home with their dog, Pete.

Mergens, Jane (Gransee) - Jane's family has been very involved with the ministry of Camp Maranatha. Her father, Louia (retired pastor of the San Diego Church), and sisters, Martha (Fernandez) and Elise (Finney), have taken leadership roles for Family Camp, Teen Camp, and Kids Kamp. Jane, as well as sisters, Cindy (Chase) and Elise, served on summer staff and all have attended as campers. Jane and her husband, Pete, live in El Cajon, California, with their daughters, Madelyne (1), and Miranda (born in October, 2001).

Miller, Debbie (Drew) - Debbie was a Kids Kamper, Teen Camper, Family Camper, Kids Kamp counselor, and craft helper. She and husband, Phil, helped in the kitchen on weekend retreats. They live in Hollidaysburg, PA, with their daughter Lauren (18), a senior in high school. They have a son, Jeffrey (24), at Cornell Medical School studying for his Ph.D. in Molecular Biology, and a daughter, Julie (22), a senior at Hofstra University on Long Island majoring in drama.

Morlan, Karrie - Karrie has served on housekeeping and kitchen staff. Her daughters, Meghan and Jana, attended Kids Kamp and Teen Camp. They live in Idyllwild, California.

Mountain Top Experience

Muska, Carol (Aulis) - From 1961 through 1970, Carol, daughter of Gerry and Alice Aulis, participated in Teen Camp, Family Camp, and Kids Kamp. She and her husband, Fran, live in Sherman, Connecticut. They have one daughter, Alexis (17).

Nelson, David "Scoop" - Scoop served on summer staff. He lives in Barbourville, Kentucky.

Novack, Emily - Emily has attended a Teen Retreat and has helped during work weekend at Camp Maranatha. She is eighteen and lives with her family in San Diego.

Oleson, Jean - Jean (or Jeannie) and her husband, Jim, lived on the camp grounds briefly and worked in food service and maintenance. Their children, Ole, Eric, Becky, and Kerry enjoyed attending camp as children and teens. Jim and Jean live in a cabin in Pine Cove, and Jean still helps out in the camp kitchen.

Paulson, Sharon - Sharon was a camper, counselor, and served on summer staff. She lives in North Hills, California.

Phan, Nghiem - Nghiem and his wife, Sherril, live in Mesa, Arizona. They have three children; Monty (28), Randy (26), and Nancy (21). Nghiem served as a staff assistant in the summer of '59.

Pitts, Ed - Ed attended Kids Kamp, Teen Camp, and Family Camp. He also served as a counselor and summer staff member. He and his wife, Marky, have three grown daughters, Pamela, Lauri, and Colleen. They live in Oceanside, California.

Rabell-Moreau, Patty - Patty attended Teen Camp and went on to work on summer staff for three years. She lives in San Diego, California, with her husband, Miles, and their children, Ian (3), and Megan (1).

About Our Contributors

Redfield, Jeremy - Jeremy, Paula (Jaffarian) Shirley's nephew, worked on summer staff. He is currently attending Bible College in Oklahoma.

Reeves, Ashly - Ashly, the daughter of Joe and Jody (Beggs) Reeves, attended Kids Kamp, Teen Camp, and Family Camp, as well as working on summer staff. She lives in Hemet, California.

Reeves, Joe and Jody (Beggs) - Jody, oldest daughter of Dick and Nancy Beggs, attended Kids Kamp, Teen Camp, and Family Camp (and "crashed" several of the guest group camps as well). She and Joe worked on summer staff as teens and year-round as adults. They are the parents of Brian (19) and Ashly (16) and live in Hemet, California.

Reid, Ralph - Ralph worked as a year-round maintenance assistant. He and his wife, Joyce, live in Idyllwild, California.

Riemenschneider, Susan - Following in the footsteps of her mother (Jewel Reimenschneider) and her uncle (David Berwanger), Susan attended several summers of Kids Kamp and then Teen Camp. She later extended her Camp Maranatha experience by joining the summer staff. Susan makes her home in Alameda, California.

Rigney, Darlene - Darlene served on summer staff and was very involved in the leadership of Teen Camp as the Advent Christian Conference Youth Director. She impacted the lives of many who were saddened by her sudden death in 1993.

Rigney, Karen - Karen attended Teen Camp and worked two summers on kitchen staff. Her sister, Darlene, and brothers, Wade and Dale, have also served on staff. She lives in Rochester, New Hampshire.

Ross, David - David is the Executive Director of the Advent Christian General Conference. He served as the main

Mountain Top Experience

speaker for several Family Camps. He and his wife live in Charlotte, North Carolina.

Sapwell, Cyndi (Walters) - Cyndi befriended the manager's daughter, Cary, as a preschooler. As an Idyllwild resident, she spent much of her childhood on the grounds of Maranatha. She attended Kids Kamp and returned from her new home in Hawaii to serve as a teen on summer staff. Cyndi lives near Adelaide, Australia, with her husband, Rupert, son, Koen, and is expecting their second child in June 2002.

Schreiner, Candee (Wright) - Candee's Camp Maranatha experience began when her dad, Earl Wright, served as the pastor of the Valley Advent Christian Church. She attended Kids Kamp, Family Camp, and Teen Camp and worked two summers on staff. Candee and husband, Tom, live in Thomaston, Georgia, with their four children, Brianna (13), Bethanie Nicholson (12), Carissa (11) and Nathan Nicholson (10). They also have two cats, Magic and Boots, and two mice, Pip and Squeak.

Scott, Lori - As a child, Lori attended camp with one of our guest groups (formerly Calvary Arrowhead, now called Inland Empire). Lori went on to serve as a counselor and staff member for that program. She lives in Riverside, California.

Shirley, Keith and Paula (Jaffarian) - Keith attended Kids Kamp, Camp Adventure (Jr. High), Teen Camp and Family Camp, along with his parents, Walt and Ruth Shirley, and brothers, Ralph and Dwight. He participated in camps as a camper, counselor and summer staff member. Paula attended Family Camp with her father (Jeff Jaffarian) and later served as a teen counselor. Keith and Paula moved to Camp Maranatha in May, 1990, where Keith has been working as the Facilities Manager. Keith and Paula live on the

About Our Contributors

grounds with their children, Timothy (16), Isaac (13) and Larissa (10).

Shirley, Ralph - Ralph (or "Ralf"—if you were on staff with him, you know what that means) attended Kids Kamp, Family Camp, and Teen Camp before serving on summer staff. He and his wife, Lois, have four children: Brian (23), Joellen (21), Bethany (12), and Michael (9). They make their home in Waterloo, Iowa.

Shirley, Walt and Ruth - Walt and Ruth have been actively involved in the ministry of Camp Maranatha since its inception and continue to volunteer their services to the camp. They have homes in Idyllwild and Hemet. Their three sons, Ralph, Dwight, and Keith, attended conference camps as children and teens, and also served on summer staff. Keith continues in full-time service at Camp Maranatha.

Sieber, Roxanna (Tate) - Roxanna first came to Camp Maranatha when her father, Joe Tom Tate, served as pastor of the Pasadena Church. She enjoyed being a Kids Kamp counselor and teacher, Teen Camper, and Family Camp participant. Roxanna's son, Daniel (now 18), traveled to Kids Kamp with his aunt and uncle (Janie and Barry Tate). Roxanna lives in Villisca, Iowa.

Snyder, Jean (Beggs) - Jean is the sister of Dick Beggs. She attended a family reunion and anniversary party for their parents which was held at Camp Maranatha. She and her husband, Gene, live in Valdosta, Georgia.

Solomon, Jonathan - Jon is an animation major at the Illinois Institute of Art. He has been a counselor and had a variety of leadership roles at Teen Camps, Teen Retreats, Kids Kamps, and Family Camps. At Kids Kamp, he is fondly known as "Nature Boy" for his role as nature teacher. He is twenty-one and currently lives in Schaumburg, IL.

Mountain Top Experience

Stiensiefer, Ken - Ken served on summer staff under Errol and Juanita Hunt. He lives and works in the Advent Christian Village in Dowling Park, Florida.

Stiers, Denise - Denise and her husband, Erik, were co-directors of Kids Kamp. Denise also counseled at Teen Camp and attended Family Camp. She and Erik live in Lancaster, California, with their children.

Tate, Barry - Barry has been a part of Camp Maranatha as a camper, staff member, and even Family Camp speaker. He and his wife, Janet (or "Janie"), have five children: Joel (28), John (26), Josh (24), Carolyn (23), and Job (22). All of them have participated in camp in a variety of ways. Barry and Janet live in Benson, Vermont.

Tate, Joel - Joel worked the summers of 1990 and 1994. He his wife, Christine, and their daughters, Elisabeth (2), and Gracie (1), also spent June and July of 2001 as an on-site staff family. They live in Wenham, Massachusetts.

Tate, John - John served on summer staff for three years ('90, '91, '92) and on the Summer Ministry Team in 1997. He lives in Benson, Vermont.

Tate, Sarah (Paulson) - Sarah first attended Family Camp as an eight-year-old with her mom and sister. She counseled at Kids Kamp and worked on summer staff as a teen and as an adult. She and her husband, Josh, live in Saint Albans, Vermont.

Underwood, Robert - Robert went to Kids Kamp and Teen Camp (not missing one year!). He served on staff in the summers of '86, '87, and '88, and as a counselor at Kids Kamp one year. He lives in Germany with his wife Mirjam. They have five children: Philip (10), Kristin-Amber (8), Christian (6), Jennifer (6), and Grace-Ariel (4).

Wade, Brian - Brian followed in the footsteps of his dad, Carl (who worked on summer staff three years as a high school student) by serving on staff for two years. He lives

About Our Contributors

with his wife, Natalie, and their son, Gavin (2) in Salt Lake City, Utah.

Wagner, Jennifer (Knott) "Jen" - Jen attended Teen Camps and retreats and worked on summer staff as a teen and as a young adult. She and her husband, Tom, live in Lemon Grove, California, with their sons, Jake (4), and Nathan (2).

Warriner, Austin - Austin and his family participated in Family Camp, Teen Camp, and Kids Kamp. He taught various classes and has served as Teen Camp Director. Austin and his wife, Dorothy, have also been camp counselors. They have two daughters, Terri Wong and Beth Danner, four grandchildren: Ashley Wong (22), Jason, Rachel, and Sara Danner (22, 16, and 13). Their first great-grandchild arrived on November 15th, 2001, Kobi Danner. The Warriners retired in 1994 (from thirty-five years of service as Advent Christian missionaries to Japan) and now live in Des Moines, Washington, happily close to all of their offspring.

Westcott, Pastor Tim - Tim is the Senior Pastor of Idyllwild Bible Church where he has served for nineteen years. He has enjoyed a long relationship with Camp Maranatha as the church and camp cooperate in ministry in Idyllwild. Pastor Tim and his wife, Lisa, have two children; Amy (16) and Brad (15).

Wilson, William - William is currently the State Director of the Youth Temperance Council (YTC), the youth division of the Woman's Christian Temperance Union. He manages a network-consulting firm in Los Angeles and is married to Josephine Nakamya Wilson. They have a son, William Jr. The family resides in Glendale, California. William attended LTL and YTC camps at Camp Maranatha throughout his childhood and youth.

Wright, Victor - Victor attended camp as a youth until he was no longer able to participate (due to a paralyzing

Mountain Top Experience

accident during a high school football game). He lives in Altadena, California.

Zimmerman, Tricia - Tricia grew up in Idyllwild, and, as her family and the Beggs family are friends, she spent time at the camp swimming and just having fun. At age sixteen, she joined the summer staff and continued working weekends in the kitchen after her summer duty was over. She lives in Goleta, California.

Illustrations

Map - Dick Beggs
Mission Statement - Jon Solomon
Dedication - Emily Novack
Acknowledgements - Ellen Koehler
Introduction - Jody Crimi
The Early Years - Jon Solomon
I Remember - Melissa Matthews
Family Camp - Janet Almon
Camp Couples - Jon Solomon
People We Recall - Graphic Rubber Stamp Co.*
Teen Camp - Melissa Matthews
Service - Jon Solomon
Guest Groups - Jon Solomon
Kids Kamp - Jon Solomon
Poet's Corner - Jon Solomon
Camp Staff - Jon Solomon
Lessons - Jon Solomon
Songs and Skits - Jon Solomon
Nature - Alvaro Favela and Graphic Rubber Stamp Co.*
Impact - Jon Solomon
Conclusion - Graphic Rubber Stamp Co.*
In Honor - Jody Crimi

About Our Contributors

*All stamp art provided by Bill and Vera Dobbs
© Graphic Rubber Stamp Co.
PO Box 340895
Arleta, Ca 91334-0895
(818) 899- 5050

Index

If you recognize some of these names and want to know how to contact a friend from the past, call or e-mail Camp Maranatha. We have a master list of names, addresses, phone numbers and e-mail addresses and will be happy to help you make a connection.

Names in bold are those for whom we do not have contact information. We would appreciate having our readers provide current information on these people so we may add it to our database.

Ainsworth, Cameron - Songs & Skits
Almon, James - People We Recall
Almon, Janet - Family Camp (Illustration)
Almon, John - Nature
Anderson, Chuck - The Early Years, Nature
Anderson, Cliff - Impact
Anderson, Frank - In Honor
Anderson, Sally - Family Camp
Anderson, Shirley - Teen Camp
Anis, Syed and Amber (Quintana) - Camp Couples
Augustine, P.H. - Family Camp
Aulis, Alice "Chief Nikomas" - In Honor
Aulis, Reverand Gerald - Family Camp, Impact, In Honor
Bailey, Pastor Bill - The Early Years
Bailey, Chuck - Impact
Bailey, Cindy (Howard) - The Early Years,* Family Camp,* People We Recall,* Kids Kamp,* Nature,* Impact*
Balser, "Buck" - Family Camp
Balser, Glendon - Family Camp
Barnes, Mrs. - Kids Kamp

Mountain Top Experience

Barths, The - People We Recall
Barth, Bob - I Remember
Barth, Melva - The Early Years
Beardsley, Sue - Service, In Honor
Beauchamp, Bette - Teen Camp
Beggs, Allison - In Honor
Beggs, Brad - Guest Groups, Lessons, In Honor
Beggs, Dick "Chief Moon" - The Early Years, I Remember, Family Camp, Camp Couples, People We Recall, Teen Camp, Service, Guest Groups, Kids Kamp, Camp Staff,* Lessons, Impact, In Honor
Beggs, Ina - Guest Groups, In Honor
Beggs, Kevin "Meatball," "Bam-Bam" - I Remember, People We Recall, Guest Groups, Camp Staff,* Lessons,* In Honor
Beggs, Nancy (Crimi) "Chief Honey"- I Remember,* Family Camp,* Camp Couples, People We Recall, Teen Camp,* Service,* Guest Groups, Kids Kamp,* Camp Staff, Lessons,* Impact, In Honor
Berdeen, Bunny - People We Recall
Bezanson, Avis - In Honor
Bezanson, Pastor Ronald - The Early Years, In Honor
Bisgard, Todd - People We Recall
Blakely, Christopher - Camp Couples, People We Recall, Teen Camp, Camp Staff
Blakely, Katherine (Fleming) - Camp Couples
Bohy, Dave - The Early Years
Bohy, Pastor Leon - The Early Years
Bottom, Kathy (Hahn) "Chicken" "Rooster"- I Remember,* People We Recall, Impact*
Bottom, Seth - Service, Impact
Bowdens, The - People We Recall
Bowden, Adlai - The Early Years, In Honor
Bowden, Katherine - In Honor
Bowden, Randy - Camp Staff*

Index

Bowse, Ron - Camp Staff
Brauer, Sherrill (Shoemaker) - Kids Kamp, Impact, In Honor
Buckleys, The - People We Recall
Bursvold, Cary (Beggs) "Little Hitler" - I Remember, Camp Couples, People We Recall, Teen Camp, Service, Guest Groups, Camp Staff,* Lessons,* Songs & Skits,* In Honor
Bursvold, Danika - In Honor
Bursvold, Jim - In Honor
Calkins, Erin - People We Recall
Campbell, Clarence - The Early Years, In Honor
Campbell, Eleanor - In Honor
Carlton, Jack(ie) - People We Recall, Kids Kamp
Carlton, Rusty - People We Recall
Carter, Pomeroy "Punk" - Camp Staff
Carter, Travis - Camp Staff
Caron (Reynolds), Saundra - People We Recall*
Cassidy, Bertha - Impact
Castleman, Kevin - People We Recall,* Teen Camp,* Kids Kamp,* Impact*
Chambers, Rolly and Ella Mae - Family Camp
Childress, Lynn - People We Recall
Christiansen, Sherry (Trivitt) - Camp Staff*
Clawitter, Debbie - People We Recall
Clean-up, General - Service
Condon, Cynthia - Camp Staff
Connelly, Carol - I Remember
Connelly, Hazel - The Early Years, In Honor
Connelly, John - The Early Years,* Impact,* In Honor*
Connelly, Leroy "Roy" - The Early Years, In Honor
Connelly, Margaret - Impact
Connelly, Ray - The Early Years
Cooper, Will - In Honor
Craig, Abby - Guest Groups*
Crawford, Bobbi - Service, Camp Staff

Mountain Top Experience

Crimis, The - I Remember, Teen Camp, Family Camp
Crimi, Betty "Chief Wawona" - The Early Years, Camp Couples, People We Recall, Teen Camp, Kids Kamp, In Honor
Crimi, Bob - The Early Years,* Camp Couples,* People We Recall,* Teen Camp, In Honor,
Crimi, Cole - In Honor
Crimi, Dave - I Remember, Camp Couples, People We Recall, Teen Camp,* Service, Camp Staff,* Lessons, Impact,* In Honor
Crimi, Gene - Family Camp,* People We Recall, Kids Kamp, In Honor
Crimi, Jim - People We Recall
Crimi, Jody - Teen Camp, In Honor* (Illustration)
Crist, Lisa - Camp Couples
Crook, Pastor Dave - Family Camp
Cruce, Sara (Summers) - Family Camp,* Service,* Kids Kamp,* Impact,* In Honor
Cruce, Tom - Family Camp, Service, Impact, In Honor
Davis, Cathie (Coe) - Poet's Corner,* Camp Staff*
Davis, Charles - Family Camp, People We Recall, Service
Davis, Jeannie - The Early Years,* Family Camp,* People We Recall,* Service,* Nature*
Davis, Jerry "Stinky" - I Remember, Camp Staff
Davis, Mary - Family Camp
Davis, Otis - Family Camp, People We Recall, Service
Davis, Samantha - Family Camp
Depew, Frank - Nature
Depew, George "Chief Moonshine" - In Honor
Depew, Mona - In Honor
DeRoche, Amy - Kids Kamp, Lessons*
DeRoche, Katie - Kids Kamp,* Camp Staff*
DeVoe, Irv - The Early Years
Dill, Lori Strauss - In Honor

Index

Dolly (the dog) - People We Recall
Douglass, Arlene - In Honor
Draper, Leota - In Honor
Draper, Sim - The Early Years, In Honor
Drew, Marie - I Remember, Kids Kamp,* Lessons,* Nature,* In Honor
Drew, Mike - Kids Kamp, In Honor
Drew, Reverend Elwell Rick "Big Chief," "Chief Golden Eagle," "Chief Bald Eagle" - The Early Years, Family Camp, Kids Kamp,* In Honor
DuFour, Jack - I Remember, Kids Kamp, Impact, In Honor
DuFour, Marilyn - Kids Kamp, In Honor
DuFour, Tim - Nature
Duke (the dog) - People We Recall
Eng, Pat "Grandma Oobie" - People We Recall
English, Tricia (Yonemoto) - Lessons*
Favela, Alvaro - Nature* (Illustration)
Favela, Liz (Dobbs) - Family Camp,* People We Recall,* Teen Camp,* Lessons,* Nature,* Impact*
Fernandez, Martha (Gransee) - Teen Camp
Finney, Elise (Gransee) - Teen Camp
Flora, Linda - I Remember
Fogle, Julie (Wilson) - Camp Staff
Foxs, The - People We Recall
Frankel, Jack - Teen Camp
Freeman, Sheri (Drew) (Hopper) - In Honor
Friedmann, Reverend Paul and Hope - In Honor
Froehlich, Bonnie (Pitts) - The Early Years,* I Remember, Camp Couples,* Kids Kamp*
Froehlich, Keith - Camp Couples
Fromhold, Adeline - Lessons, In Honor
Fromhold, Carl - The Early Years, Family Camp, Lessons, In Honor
Gama, Ben - People We Recall
Gama, Gabe - People We Recall

Mountain Top Experience

Gandy, Gladys - In Honor
Gardner, Anna Mae - People We Recall,* Service,* Nature*
Gilbert, Christina (Parker) - Camp Couples,* People We Recall,* Impact*
Gilbert, Micah - Camp Couples
Gillogly, Carolyn (Schenk) - People We Recall,* Teen Camp,* Songs & Skits,* In Honor*
Glen, Steve - In Honor
Glovers, Robert and Margaret - Teen Camp, In Honor
Gosnell, Amy - People We Recall
Gransee, Louia - Family Camp
Gransees, The - Family Camp
Grey, Bill "Big Bird" - Teen Camp
Gustafson, Tim - Impact
Gustafson, Zann - I Remember, Poet's Corner
Hagin, Amy (Gustafson) - People We Recall
Hammond, Debbie (Peckens) - I Remember,* People We Recall,* Teen Camp,* Songs & Skits*
Hardi, Dean - Camp Staff*
Harris, Brandi - People We Recall
Hay, Laura - Guest Groups*
Henneberry, Jeanette (Schenk) - People We Recall,* Songs & Skits*
Hogan, Janie (Hill) - Camp Staff*
Hopper, Rob "Robby" - Kids Kamp,* Nature,* In Honor*
Howard, Charles - People We Recall
Howard, Gardner - Family Camp
Howard, Norma "Chief Red Squirrel" - People We Recall
Hunts, The - I Remember, People We Recall, Family Camp, Nature
Hunt, Erroll - The Early Years, Camp Couples, People We Recall, Service, Camp Staff, Impact, in Honor
Hunt, Juanita - The Early Years, Camp Couples, People We Recall, Service, Camp Staff, Lessons, Impact

Index

Hutchins, Leslie (McIver) - Teen Camp,* Kids Kamp*
Hutchins, Paul - Camp Staff,* Nature*
Ironfield, Derri (Knowles) - Poet's Corner,* Camp Staff,* Impact*
Jackson, Claudia (Smith) - Family Camp
Jackson, Jamie "Jamo" - People We Recall,* Kids Kamp,* Camp Staff*
Jackson, Liz "Chief Red Fox" - People We Recall
Jaffarian, Caitlin "Katie" "Short Stop" - Family Camp
Jaffarian, Calvin - Camp Staff,* People
Jaffarian, Dickey - The Early Years
Jaffarian, Ed "Uncle Buddy" - The Early Years, Family Camp, In Honor
Jaffarian, Flo - People We Recall
Jaffarian, Grant - People We Recall, Poet's Corner, Camp Staff, Impact*
Jaffarian, Michael - Family Camp
Jaffarian, Myron - The Early Years
Jaffarian, Paul "Jeff" - The Early Years,* Family Camp,* People We Recall
Jaffarian, P.H. - Family Camp, People We Recall
Jaffarian, Rogers - Family Camp
Jaffarian, Ruby - The Early Years, In Honor
Jaffarian, Tara - People We Recall
Jandayan, Jane (Palmer) - Family Camp
Johnson, Jerry - The Early Years
Johnson, Marco - Camp Staff
Johnson, Michelle - Camp Staff*
Judy, Dan - Impact
Kelly, Katie (Cruce) - Family Camp, People We Recall,* Teen Camp, Kids Kamp, Impact,* In Honor
Knapp, Ron - Teen Camp
Knechtels, The - Family Camp
Knechtel, Elizabeth "Smitty" - Family Camp, In Honor

Mountain Top Experience

Koehler, Beth - I Remember, Teen Camp, Songs & Skits
Koehler, Bill - Kids Kamp
Koehler, Ellen - Family Camp,* Teen Camp,* Kids Kamp,* Songs & Skits,* Acknowledgements (Illustration), Nature,* Impact,* In Honor*
Koehler, Lillian - I Remember, Family Camp, People We Recall, Teen Camp, Service, Songs & Skits, Impact, In Honor
Koehler, Sheldon - People We Recall,* Teen Camp,* Kids Kamp*, Songs & Skits,* Nature*
Krueger, Matt - Camp Staff*
Kuhn, Vickie - I Remember
Ladd, Dr. (Pastor) George and Mrs. - The Early Years
Laroche, Carol (Peckens) - I Remember,* Songs & Skits,* Nature,* Impact*
Laroche, Sara - Impact
Lay, Clark - In Honor
Lay, Steve - Impact
Lay, Tim - Camp Staff
Lazar, Denny - Camp Couples, Service
Lazar, Shannon (Wickens) - Camp Couples, Service, Camp Staff
Linscott, Scott - Impact
Lobb, Aleta - In Honor
Lobb, Lois - Kids Kamp
Luton, Dorothy - People We Recall, Service
Lynch, Noah - Camp Staff*
Mansfield, Della - Family Camp
Mansfield, Paul - Impact
March, Al "Beanie" - People We Recall,* Camp Staff, Impact*
March, Paula - People We Recall
Mark, Pastor Les - Teen Camp, Impact
Marron, Gwen (Koehler) - I Remember,* Family Camp,* People We Recall,* Teen Camp,* Songs & Skits,* Impact*

Index

Marshall, Greg - Camp Staff
Matthews, Carol - People We Recall
Matthews, Chuck - People We Recall
Matthews, Melissa - People We Recall,* Service,* Camp Staff,* Impact*
McCaghren, Holly (Plummer) - Camp Couples,* Lessons (2)*
McCaghren, Scott - Camp Couples
McGath, Kay (Mooneyham) - Impact
McGregor, Dini (Walters) - I Remember,* Family Camp, Kids Kamp,* Songs & Skits, Impact*
McIver, Marilyn - Kids Kamp*
McIver, Paul - People We Recall, Kids Kamp, Camp Staff
McKinley, Misty (Wilson)- People We Recall
Meeker, Danny - The Early Years
Mellor, Ken - In Honor
Mellor, Olga - Impact
Menish, Judy (Hall) "Schultze" - The Early Years,* I Remember,* Impact*
Mergens, Jane (Gransee) - Camp Couples,* Poet's Corner,* Songs & Skits*
Mergens, Pete - Camp Couples
Miller, Debbie (Drew) "Chief Chickadee" - I Remember,* Family Camp,* Camp Couples,* Kids Kamp,* Songs & Skits,* Nature,* In Honor
Miller, Lori - People We Recall
Miller, Phil - I Remember, Camp Couples
Mills, Ray and Jennie - People We Recall
Moore, Cindy (Chase) - Family Camp
Moose (the dog) - People We Recall
Morlan, Pastor Bruce - Guest Groups
Morlan, Karrie - Service,* Guest Groups*
Mosgar, Jana - I Remember
Murphy, Darci - Camp Staff

Mountain Top Experience

Murphy, Lyn - Camp Staff
Mushrush, Edith - Family Camp, In Honor
Mushrush, Floyd - In Honor
Muska, Carol (Aulis) - I Remember,* Family Camp,* Camp Couples,* People We Recall,* Teen Camp,* In Honor
Nelson, David "Scoop" - Impact*
"Norman" - I Remember, Camp Staff, Lessons
Novack, Emily - Dedication* (Illustration)
Oleson, Jeannie - Service, Camp Staff*
Osborn, Robby - Songs & Skits
Osborne, Pastor - The Early Years
Palmer, Carol - People We Recall
Palmer, John - The Early Years, People We Recall
Panda (the dog) - Lessons
Parker, Lynn - Teen Camp
Parolini, Roger - I Remember, Family Camp
Paulson, Sharon - Camp Staff*
Perry, Mrs. "Chief Nikomas" - Kids Kamp
Peterson, Roy and Estelle - The Early Years
Phan, Nghiem and Sherril - I Remember*
Pitts, The - Family Camp
Pitts, Ed - The Early Years*
Pitts, Harry - The Early Years, In Honor
Pitts, Marj - Kids Kamp
Rabell-Moreau, Patty - Poet's Corner,* Impact*
Redfield, Jeremy - People We Recall, Camp Staff*
Redfield, Margaret Chambers - Family Camp
Reed, John - In Honor
Reeves, Ashly - I Remember, People We Recall, Kids Kamp, Camp Staff, Lessons,* In Honor
Reeves, Brian - I Remember, People We Recall, Camp Staff, In Honor
Reeves, Jody (Beggs) - The Early Years,* I Remember, Family Camp,* Camp Couples,* People We Recall,* People We

Index

Recall, Service,* Guest Groups,* Kids Kamp,* Poet's Corner,* Camp Staff, Lessons* (Three Sisters), Lessons,* Songs & Skits, Impact,* In Honor
Reeves, Joe - People We Recall, Poet's Corner,* In Honor
Reid, Ralph - People We Recall,* Camp Staff,* Impact*
Rice, Pastor Chet - The Early Years
Richard, Lisa - Camp Staff
Richardson, "Old Man" - The Early Years
Riemenschneider, Susan - Poet's Corner,* Impact*
Rigney, Brad - Teen Camp
Rigney, Darlene Marie - Camp Couples, People We Recall, Teen Camp, Service, Poet's Corner,* Impact, In Honor
Rigney, Karen - Poet's Corner*
Rolands III, Cedro - Impact
Sanderson, Jon - Teen Camp
Sanderson, Nathan - People We Recall
Sapwell, Cyndi (Walters) - Kids Kamp,* Impact
Schmekel, Al - The Early Years, In Honor
Schmekel, Betty - In Honor
Schmekel, Ethel - In Honor
Schmekel, Glenn - Impact
Schreiner, Candee (Wright) - People We Recall,* Poet's Corner,* Camp Staff,* Nature*
Scotts, The - People We Recall
Scott, Brittany - Guest Groups
Scott, Pastor Frank - The Early Years, In Honor
Scott, Larry - Guest Groups
Scott, Lori - Guest Groups*
Shea, Mike - Family Camp, People We Recall, Camp Staff
Shelton, Everal - Kids Kamp
Sherry, Lisa - Teen Camp
Sherry, Rod - Teen Camp, Songs & Skits
Shirleys, The - Teen Camp
Shirley, David - People We Recall

Mountain Top Experience

Shirley, Dwight - Family Camp, People We Recall, Teen Camp, Camp Staff
Shirley, Isaac - Family Camp, People We Recall, Service, Camp Staff, Impact
Shirley, Keith - I Remember, Family Camp, Camp Couples, People We Recall, Service, Guest Groups, Camp Staff,* Nature,* Impact, In Honor
Shirley, Larissa - People We Recall, Service, Camp Staff, Impact
Shirley, Paula (Jaffarian) - I Remember, Family Camp,* Camp Couples,* People We Recall,* Service,* Guest Groups, Camp Staff, Impact, In Honor
Shirley, Ralph - Family Camp, Teen Camp, Camp Staff, Impact*
Shirley, Ruth - The Early Years, I Remember,* Family Camp,* Teen Camp, Service,* Camp Staff,* Impact*
Shirley, Timothy - Family Camp, People We Recall, Service, Camp Staff, Impact
Shirley, Walt - The Early Years,* Family Camp, Teen Camp,* Service,* Camp Staff,* Lessons*
Shoemakers, The - Family Camp
Shoemaker, Earl - In Honor
Shoemaker, Wesley - Camp Staff
Shoemaker, Yvonne - In Honor
Shuman, Mark - People We Recall
Shuman, Pastor Phil "Uncle Phil" - The Early Years, People We Recall, Teen Camp, In Honor
Sieber, Roxanna (Tate) - Teen Camp,* Nature*
Slater, Chris - Teen Camp
Slusser, Michael "Mike" - People We Recall, Teen Camp
Smiths, The - Family Camp
Smith, Andy - Family Camp, People We Recall
Smith (?), Jack - Kids Kamp
Smith, Pastor Jim - I Remember, Kids Kamp, Impact

Index

Smith, Mark - Nature
Smith, Sylvia - Family Camp
Snyder, Kris (Combs) - People We Recall
Snyder, Jean (Beggs) - Guest Groups*
Solomon, Jon "Nature Boy" - The Early Years,* Camp Couples,* Service,* Guest Groups,* Kids Kamp,* Poet's Corner,* Camp Staff,* Lessons,* Songs & Skits* (Illustrations)
Stansbury, Leann - Nature
Steinseifer, Ken "Kenny" "Head-a-Hopper" - The Early Years,* I Remember, People We Recall,* Camp Staff,* Impact*
Stiers, Denise - Family Camp,* People We Recall,* Teen Camp,* Kids Kamp,* Poet's Corner*
Stiers, Erik - People We Recall, Kids Kamp
Stiers, Joshua - Kids Kamp
Summers, Scott - People We Recall
Tamminga, Denise - Guest Groups
Tapley, Anna (McGath) - Camp Couples, People We Recall
Tapley, Dave - Family Camp, Camp Couples, People We Recall, Songs & Skits
Tapley, Kim - People We Recall
Tapley, Mike - Camp Couples, People We Recall, Songs & Skits
Tate, Barry Joe - The Early Years,* People We Recall,* Camp Staff, Impact
Tate, Christine - Camp Staff
Tate, Elizabeth - Camp Staff
Tate, Gracie - Camp Staff
Tate, Job - Camp Staff
Tate, Joe Tom - Family Camp, Teen Camp, Camp Staff
Tate, Joel "Dunderhead" - Camp Staff, Lessons*
Tate, John - Camp Staff,* Nature
Tate, Josh "Captain of Industry" - Camp Couples, Camp Staff

Mountain Top Experience

Tate, Sarah (Paulson) - Camp Couples, People We Recall, Service,* Camp Staff
Taylor, Barbie (Smith) - I Remember, Kids Kamp
Taylor, Harold and Bertha - In Honor
Theile, Chris - Guest Groups
Theile, John - Guest Groups
Thunderbird, Chief - Kids Kamp, In Honor
Titus, Ruth - People We Recall
Tyler, Becky - People We Recall
Underwood, Robert - People We Recall,* Service,* Kids Kamp,* Camp Staff,* Nature
Vadman, Diane - Teen Camp
Wade, Brian - Impact*
Wagner, Jennifer (Knott) - Lessons,* Songs & Skits,* Impact
Warriner, Austin - The Early Years*
Warriner, Dorothy - The Early Years
Westcott, Pastor Tim - Guest Groups*
White, Janet (Fletcher) - Impact
Wickens, Mark and Sherry (Foutz) - Camp Couples
Wilson, Colleen M. - Guest Groups
Wilson, William L. - Guest Groups*
Wolf, Norberto - Guest Groups
Woodgate, Ginny - Teen Camp
Woodgate, Vernon - In Honor
Wright, David - People We Recall
Wright, Earl - The Early Years, People We Recall
Wright, Victor - Impact*
Yost, David - People We Recall
Zimmerman, Tricia - I Remember,* Lessons*

*Indicates an entry written or illustrated by this person

To order additional copies of

MOUNTAIN TOP
Experience

Call Camp Maranatha

at (909) 659-2739

for ordering information

More Camp Memories . . .